SUSTAINA *is fo* EVERYO

BEGINNING S
to CREATINC
SUSTAINABIL
PROGRAM *f*
YOUR BUSINE

SUSTAINABILITY
is for
EVERYONE

BEGINNING STEPS *to* CREATING *a* SUSTAINABILITY PROGRAM *for* YOUR BUSINESS

LAEL GIEBEL

Accomplishing Innovation Press
1497 Main St. Suite 169
Dunedin, FL 34698
accomplishinginnovationpress.com
AccomplishingInnovationPress@gmail.com

Cover by Accomplishing Innovation Press
Typesetting by Autumn Skye
Edited by Joseph Mistretta

Library of Congress Control Number: 2022945435

Paperback ISBN-13: 979-8-8232-0059-2
Hardcover ISBN-13: 978-1-64450-731-5
Audiobook ISBN-13: 979-8-8232-0052-3
Ebook ISBN-13: 979-8-8232-0058-5

DEDICATION:

For my family, friends, and all life that calls this beautiful green and blue globe 'home'.

"A useful definition of sustainability is, "being able continue what you are doing for the next 1,000 years without destroying, or seriously disrupting the natural environment that supports us all." Lael Giebel has applied the wide-ranging concepts of an ecological generalist to the specific field of community and corporate sustainability, and from within the traditionally difficult operating circumstances of the bureaucratic world, she has consistently crafted practical, educational responses to basic issues facing us today. A much needed orderly and pragmatic guide."

Phil Hawes, Ph.D
Author of "The EcoVillage Design-Build Handbook: Creating
Sustainable Human-Ecosystems"
Architect, Biosphere II

"Finally, a practical guide to organizational sustainability that can work for any public, private or non-profit enterprise. The author breaks down a complex existential problem into manageable initiatives that can be adopted by any organization. Ms. Giebel tackles the paralyzing fear of extinction with a calming roadmap to organizational sustainability."

Gregory A. Rice, M.A, M.B.A
Community Development Director
City of Inverness, Florida

"Lael Giebel's approach to sustainability is at once both pragmatic and comprehensive. Her passion for the environment, coupled with her education and experience make her an effective leader in the industry."

Graham Hill
Founder, CEO
TreeHugger.com, LifeEdited, The Carbonauts

Sustainability is for Everyone is sure to become a "must read" for any organization looking to incorporate sustainability measures into their business practices or reduce its environmental footprint. The book is to be commended for its straightforward, no-nonsense approach, and absence of industry-specific jargon. Its usefulness comes from the clear suggestions that are backed by real world examples, and nearly everything suggested in the book can be easily implemented.

Professor Victoria A. Beard, Cornell University
Inaugural Director, Cornell Mui Ho Center for Cities
Fellow, World Resources Institute

"Lael Giebel is one of the true crusaders to make a change for our world. Her knowledge on the subject and dedication is praiseworthy. I have had the amazing opportunity to work with her as she established and grew sustainability programs. Her passion and drive make her a true environmental warrior. Every company needs to do this."

Erika Lance, CEO

Contents

Introduction

$\mathcal{I}$ want to begin by offering a definition of sustainability. While there are varied definitions, the main one accepted by the industry, which I like for its simplicity, is this: *sustainability means meeting our own needs without compromising the ability of future generations to meet their own needs.* This most definitely covers the environment, but also includes social and economic aspects. I will leave the definition at that, as I don't want this to turn into a theoretical discussion. I very much want this book to be a practical tool for any company or organization to use. There is ample discussion on the internet regarding sustainability and its three principles or four pillars (the differences of which are more an issue of semantics than of content). I would encourage anyone with an interest to dive deeper, as there really is some good information online and in published works.

Roadmap

This book is meant to act as a roadmap of sorts. Consider it the ABCs of starting a sustainability program. In that vein, throughout the book, I will refer to a mythical ABC Company to provide examples. What I offer here is a hands-on approach to implementing a sustainability program in any organization (public, private, government, non-profit, etc.), regardless of size or length of time in business. If you are looking for a simple way to "check" the sustainability box, then this book probably isn't for you. But if you are looking for meaningful ways to make your business operations more sustainable, and to include your employees on your journey, then please read on.

While I call this book a roadmap, the order in which you implement these steps is not crucial and is actually quite flexible. Similarly, you do not need to implement each of these steps. Take what works for your organization and your company culture and start there. If some of the suggestions listed here do not fit for now, then maybe they will later. Or maybe they will never be relevant, in which case you can dismiss them entirely.

I also want to address ESGs just momentarily. According to the website Robeco, ESG means using Environmental, Social, and Governance factors to evaluate companies and countries on how far advanced they are with sustainability. So, within the next few years, and possibly even within the next year, ESGs, or some form of ESG reporting, will likely be required for public companies. This book is not about how to meet those requirements. Instead, this book is about how to incorporate an enriching and impactful sustainability program into your company.

Just Start

The best advice I can probably give you regarding your program is to just start. Start somewhere. If you are not ready to take on all of this, then just take on one thing. You can take baby steps or make revolutionary changes; do what works for you and your organization. Don't let staff constraints or time limitations stop you from embarking on your sustainability journey – do at least one thing!

Another thing I want to point out at the onset, and will mention again in various chapters, is that different states and countries do things differently. I know, that was painfully obvious. What I mean is, keep in mind, for instance, that the way you recycle in your home office may (and likely will) be different than how recycling is handled in other states and nations and even in different cities within your state. It may even be different than how your employees recycle at home, depending on your solid waste collectors. That applies to more than just recycling and is something to keep in mind, particularly if you have offices in more than one location.

Benefits of a Sustainability Program

It is also important to discuss the reasons for and benefits of implementing a sustainability program, which are many. I will start with the obvious: it is the right thing to do! Many of us know this at a gut level, if not an intellectual one. In his article titled, "Caring for the Environment: 8 Reasons to Protect & Sustain Earth," John McCloy mentions the following reasons it is important to protect the environment, which many of us inherently recognize as true:

- We Only Have One Earth as Our Home

- Clean Environment Means Healthier Lives

- Rise in the Overall Earth's Temperatures

- Caring For the Environment Protects the Ecosystem and Humanity

- Biodiversity is Essential

- The Environment Provides Various Raw Materials and Habitats

- We Have a Moral Obligation

- Protecting the Environment is an Excellent Way to Give Back

But having said that, there are many people for whom this is not true, so this cannot be the only reason to run your business sustainably.

I think the next most obvious reason is public perception. More and more, customers, vendors, residents, stakeholders, and investors are asking about, if not demanding, sustainability measures. I believe this will only continue and increase in the foreseeable future. If customers and investors have a choice between two essentially equal companies, and one has its sustainability program in place, and one does not, guess which one they more frequently will pick? If you said the one with its sustainability measures established, you are correct.

There is another big benefit to implementing your sustainability program. Your attention to the environment will also make you more attractive to potential employees. You might be surprised by how important it is. According to a report by PWC titled "The future of work: A journey to 2022", 65 percent of people in the U.S., Germany, India, China, and the U.K. want to work for an organization with a strong social conscience. According to the online magazine *Worklife,* new research (as of 2021) from global recruitment firm Robert Walters indicates 34 percent of U.K. office workers would refuse a job offer if a company's environmental, sustainability, or climate control values do not align with their own. In the U.S., the figure is even higher: 41 percent. France and Chile (both at 53 percent) top the list, closely followed by Switzerland (52 percent). This will only increase over time. I have found this to be anecdotally true in my own experience, as well.

Personal Introduction

Finally, I want to let you know who I am and how I came to write this book. I came by my passion for the environment naturally. I was born to hippie-hearted parents who taught me to love and respect the natural world. They were both raised in Asia in the 40s and 50s when resources were quite limited. As a result, I grew up virtually wasting nothing; my mom reused nearly everything, we only shopped in used clothing stores, we grew vegetables and then composted the scraps, we saved yogurt containers and reused them for storage, etc. The first time my mom saw my now husband grab two paper towels to dry his hands after washing them, and then throw the paper towels away, she nearly lost her mind! Thankfully my husband has since joined me in the ways of environmentally friendly behavior.

As a child, I spent my summers on an island in Maine with no running water, no electricity, no phones, and no cars. And it was heavenly. It is still my favorite place on earth. In fact, one of my first memories was landing on the island when I was a little over two years old. When my dad remarried, his new wife (my bonus mom for over 40 years now) brought with her the same reverence for the environment and shared our love of the island. It was a given that we lived in harmony with the environment, rather than battling or abusing it.

On a professional level, I worked early on for a clothing manufacturer that made design history as the first U.S. company to create a clothing line made entirely of hemp; unheard of at the time. They were leaders in the eco-clothing market and ran their company sustainably before most people had heard of the term. More recently, I worked for a local city government for 16 years before moving to the corporate environment. Inspired by my lifelong passion for environmental conservation, I became a LEED AP (Leadership in Energy and Environmental Design, Accredited Professional) in 2009, about five years into my government career. Two years later, I received my MBA in Sustainability. While at the city government, I co-authored and subsequently re-engineered the first green building code. I was the staff lead on several green building projects and was responsible for setting increasingly ambitious energy goals, including committing to both the Sierra Club's Ready For 100 (100% clean energy by 2035) and upholding the Paris Climate Agreement goals. Our city also became the first city to achieve Platinum level certification as a Florida Local Green Government in 2019. I became a certified TRUE (Total Resource Use and Efficiency) Advisor in 2021, which means I am trained in zero waste management to help companies meet their waste goals and cut their carbon footprint. I also hold several other green certifications.

When I left the government and took my initial corporate position as Director of Facility Services and Sustainability, I had a long list of sustainability targets and initiatives I wanted to accomplish and the freedom and support to do so. I cannot stress enough how powerful this was. I got the green light (and the support needed along with the thumbs-up) for each of my ideas, with no stops or hurdles to overcome. The switch from the theoretical (policies, legislative priorities, etc.) to the practical (establishing a green team, putting a recycling program into place, etc.) was much easier than I had expected and was quite satisfying. That being said, there was no roadmap for me to follow, just a collection of ideas I had been chewing on for years and was finally able to put into action. Several times a friend of mine encouraged me to write a book on sustainability; this book. Each time I shrugged it off or dismissed her nudges.

At one point, I did a series of presentations on sustainability and ESGs for our senior- level executives. After one of those presentations, one of the executives said that "we do more for sustainability here than at any company I have ever worked for. And those have all been California companies." California is typically at the forefront of sustainability initiatives, so this was really saying something. I was quite struck when he said that. Well, okay, I was beaming with pride when he said that! But it also stuck with me. So the next time my friend suggested that I write a book on sustainability, I decided that maybe I did have something to say. And from there came this book.

My intention with writing this book is to get you moving quickly, because there is no need to reinvent the wheel. Is this book exhaustive? No, there are plenty more ideas out there, and I am sure those ideas and innovations will continue to expand. But this will get you started and will hopefully take some of the guesswork and stumbling out of the process. I do want to mention that the Green Business Bureau has put out a useful document called "The Sustainability Checklist: 25 Things To Do when Launching and Managing a Sustainability Program". It may be a good compliment to this book.

State of the Environment

W hile this is a solutions-oriented book, I wanted to start off by covering some of the environmental issues of the day. I will spend the rest of the book discussing ways to make your company more sustainable, which will ultimately address most, if not all of these. So if you start to feel a bit discouraged reading these, fear not. By even picking this book up, you have decided you will be a part of the solution, so take heart in that.

Waste

Let's start by looking at the wasted resources that are literally accumulating around us in the form of landfills. Landfills are where any waste that is not recycled or reused goes to die, as it were. It is where garbage is dumped and left to accumulate. According to the Environmental Protection Agency (EPA), in 2018, about 146.1 million tons of waste was landfilled in the United States alone, rather than being reused, recycled, repurposed, composted, or upcycled. Food was the largest component at about 24 percent. Plastics accounted for over 18 percent, paper and paperboard made up about 12 percent, and rubber, leather, and textiles comprised over 11 percent. Other materials accounted for less than 10 percent each. Good news alert: Landfilling of waste has decreased from 94 percent of the amount generated in 1960 to 50 percent of the amount generated in 2018. That's something to celebrate right now, and you haven't even gotten into the solutions part of the book! But let's not get ahead of ourselves just yet.

One thing to take particular note of is food waste, which makes up 24 percent of the landfill. Perhaps even more shocking is that according to the National Resources Defense Council (NRDC), Up to 40 percent of the food in the United States is never eaten. One issue with food waste is that an enormous amount of resources and energy go into growing, processing, transporting, and eventually disposing of all that wasted food. That includes climate-wrecking greenhouse gas emissions at every stage of the food system, plus water, fertilizer, packaging, labor, and more. But in addition to that, when food goes to the landfill and rots, it produces methane—a greenhouse gas even more potent than carbon dioxide. So it behooves each of us to try to tackle this issue, at least on a personal level, by first wasting less food, and then by composting, rather than throwing away food. This will be revisited in Chapter 3, Waste Management.

In addition to food waste, trash in general, and landfills in particular, are a real issue. Landfills are a waste of, well, land, and are also unsightly and often smelly. Unfortunately, they are also a major source of pollution. According to an article on Unisan's website titled, "What is a landfill? Why are landfills bad for the environment?", the three main problems with landfills are toxins, leachate, and greenhouse gasses. Many materials that end up as waste, such as electronics, contain toxic substances. Organic waste produces bacteria which break the rubbish down. The decaying waste produces weak acidic chemicals which combine with liquids in the waste to form leachate (the liquid formed when waste breaks down in the landfill and water filters through that waste). This liquid is highly toxic and can pollute land, groundwater, and waterways. And finally, according to Unisan, greenhouse gas production is perhaps the biggest environmental threat posed by landfills. When organic material, such as food scraps and green waste, is put in landfills, it is generally compacted down and covered. This removes the oxygen and causes it to break down in an anaerobic process. Eventually, this releases methane, a greenhouse gas that is about 25 times more potent than carbon dioxide. Landfill gas comprises 35-55 percent methane and 30-44 percent carbon dioxide.

We hear a lot about pollution, but just what is so bad about it? Read on for some sobering information on pollution from the Department of Environmental Protection (DEP).

Health: People exposed to high enough levels of certain air pollutants may experience:

• Irritation of the eyes, nose, and throat

• Wheezing, coughing, chest tightness, and breathing difficulties

• Worsening of existing lung and heart problems, such as asthma

• Increased risk of heart attack

In addition, long-term exposure to air pollution can cause cancer and damage to the immune, neurological, reproductive, and respiratory systems. In extreme cases, it can even cause death.

Environmental effects:

• Acid rain is precipitation containing harmful amounts of nitric and sulfuric acids. In the environment, acid rain damages trees and causes soils and water bodies to acidify, making the water unsuitable for some fish and other wildlife. It also speeds the decay of buildings, statues, and sculptures that are part of our national heritage.

- Eutrophication is a condition in a body of water where high concentrations of nutrients (such as nitrogen) stimulate blooms of algae, which in turn can cause fish to die and the loss of plant and animal diversity. Although eutrophication is a natural process in the aging of lakes and some estuaries, human activities can greatly accelerate eutrophication by increasing the rate at which nutrients enter aquatic ecosystems. Air emissions of nitrogen oxides from power plants, cars, trucks, and other sources contribute to the amount of nitrogen entering aquatic ecosystems.

- Haze is caused when sunlight encounters tiny pollution particles in the air. Haze obscures the clarity, color, texture, and form of what we see. Some haze-causing pollutants (mostly fine particles) are directly emitted to the atmosphere by sources such as power plants, industrial facilities, trucks and automobiles, and construction activities. Others are formed when gasses emitted into the air (such as sulfur dioxide and nitrogen oxides) form particles as they are carried downwind.

- Effects on wildlife. Toxic pollutants in the air, or deposited on soils or surface waters, can impact wildlife in a number of ways. Like humans, animals can experience health problems if they are exposed to sufficient concentrations of air toxins over time. Studies show that air toxins are contributing to birth defects, reproductive failure, and disease in animals. Persistent toxic air pollutants (those that break down slowly in the environment) are of particular concern in aquatic ecosystems. These pollutants accumulate in sediments and may biomagnify in tissues of animals at the top of the food chain to concentrations many times higher than in the water or air.

- Ozone depletion. Ozone is a gas that occurs both at ground level and in the earth's upper atmosphere, known as the stratosphere. At ground level, ozone is a pollutant that can harm human health. In the stratosphere, however, ozone forms a layer that protects life on earth from the sun's harmful ultraviolet (UV) rays. But this "good" ozone is gradually being destroyed by man-made chemicals referred to as ozone-depleting substances, including chlorofluorocarbons, hydrochlorofluorocarbons, and halons. Thinning of the protective ozone layer can cause increased amounts of UV radiation to reach the earth, which can lead to more cases of skin cancer, cataracts, and impaired immune systems. UV can also damage sensitive crops, such as soybeans, and reduce crop yields.

- Crop and forest damage. Air pollution can damage crops and trees in a variety of ways. Ground-level ozone can lead to reductions in agricultural crop and commercial forest yields, reduced growth and survivability of tree seedlings, and increased plant susceptibility to disease, pests, and other environmental stresses (such as harsh weather). As described above, crop and forest damage can also result from acid rain and from increased UV radiation caused by ozone depletion.

Air pollution contributes to 11.65% of deaths globally.

– Our World in Data

Deforestation

Most people can probably agree that forests are pretty glorious and worth protecting. But I will turn to the World Wildlife Fund (WWF) for just why it is so important that we protect them: As well as being stunningly beautiful, forests are vital for the health of our planet. They provide food and shelter for so much of life on earth – from fungi and insects to tigers and elephants. More than half the world's land-based plants and animals, and three-quarters of all birds, live in and around forests. Forests have a big influence on rainfall patterns, water and soil quality, and flood prevention. Millions of people rely directly on forests as their home or for making a living.

But the risks from deforestation go even wider. In fact, they are often referred to as the "lungs of the planet" because they draw in carbon dioxide and breathe out oxygen. If forests are cleared, or even disturbed, they release carbon dioxide and other greenhouse gasses. Forest loss and damage is the cause of around 10 percent of global warming. There's simply no way we can fight the climate crisis if we don't stop deforestation. According to ThoughtCo, a mature leafy tree produces as much oxygen in a season as 10 people inhale in a year. That alone is a compelling reason to protect and/or plant trees, since all of us are exceedingly fond of breathing.

The Humane League further points out that deforestation's environmental impact extends far beyond the edges of the woods. When we remove forests, we lose out on the vital protection they provide against climate change, soil erosion, and natural disasters like flooding. And deforestation, along with other human activities such as industrial agriculture and the burning of fossil fuels, accelerates ocean acidification (when the ocean absorbs CO_2, lowering the water's pH level and making it more acidic).

Finally, deforestation is devastating to wildlife. According to StandforTrees.org, deforestation affects animals in many ways. It causes habitat destruction, resulting in the loss of their homes, or being forced out of their natural range. Deforestation results in reduced food availability and increased risk of predation by removing sources of shelter, water, and food, such as fruit-bearing trees. Animal species threatened by forest loss may also face increased competition with others and can be at higher risk of being killed by predators who have also lost their natural habitat. The impacts of deforestation may be direct or indirect, but the end result is the same: population decrease and higher risk of extinction. In fact, deforestation is one of the main causes of extinction.

In the time it takes to say 'deforestation', another chunk of forest the size of a football pitch is destroyed.

– World Wildlife Fund, UK

Ocean acidification

Ocean acidification is literally causing a sea change that is threatening the fundamental chemical balance of ocean and coastal waters from pole to pole. According to NOAA Fisheries, ocean acidification is sometimes called "osteoporosis of the sea." Ocean acidification can create conditions that eat away at the minerals used by oysters, clams, lobsters, shrimp, coral reefs, and other marine life to build their shells and skeletons. Beyond sea life, this also affects human health. According to the same NOAA article, in the laboratory, many harmful algal species produce more toxins and bloom faster in acidified waters. A similar response in the wild could harm people eating contaminated shellfish and sicken fish and marine mammals. And while ocean acidification won't make seawater dangerous for swimming, it will upset the balance among the multitudes of microscopic life found in every drop of seawater. Such changes can affect seafood supplies and the ocean's ability to store pollutants, including future carbon emissions.

In recent decades, ocean acidification has been occurring 100 times faster than during natural events over the past 55 million years.

– European Environment Agency

Global Climate Change

I do not want to dwell too long on climate change, because I know this is still a hot topic among many (trite pun intended). It certainly deserves discussion, however. According to the Department of Environmental Protection (DEP), the earth's atmosphere contains a delicate balance of naturally occurring gasses that trap some of the sun's heat near the earth's surface. This "greenhouse effect" keeps the earth's temperature stable. Unfortunately, evidence is mounting that humans have disturbed this natural balance by producing large amounts of some of these greenhouse gasses, including carbon dioxide and methane. As a result, the earth's atmosphere appears to be trapping more of the sun's heat, causing the earth's average temperature to rise - a phenomenon known as global warming. Many scientists believe that global warming could have significant impacts on human health, agriculture, water resources, forests, wildlife, and coastal areas.

Not everyone agrees that climate change is caused by humans, but I think most people can agree that even if we didn't *cause* climate change, we can certainly attempt to live and operate in a way that does not exacerbate it. By implementing a sustainability program as outlined in this book, you are doing your part to not exacerbate climate change. See chapters 3 and 4, Waste Management and Measure Your Carbon Footprint, respectively, for more on how to reduce your impact on the environment and climate.

Methane is the primary contributor to the formation of ground-level ozone, a hazardous air pollutant and greenhouse gas, exposure to which causes 1 million premature deaths every year. Methane is also a powerful greenhouse gas. Over a 20-year period, it is 80 times more potent at warming than carbon dioxide.

– UN Environment Programme

Philanthropy

By applying the many suggestions in this book you are going a long way in taking responsibility for the environment and mitigating the many issues mentioned above. Another way to contribute to a solution, and feel good while doing it, is to include the environment in your philanthropic efforts. Consider donating to have trees planted or organize a tree planting effort with your staff. Look into adopting beehives, or other wildlife, or a section of a park or forest. Perhaps you could donate to support cleaning up ocean garbage (such as the Great Pacific Garbage Patch), or organize beach cleanups with your employees.

"Look in the mirror, consider your talents, and think about how you might use them to make a difference. Some have artistic skills, others are good with numbers or have a way with words. Everyone has power to make a difference as an individual, or by joining the company of others who share a common goal. The key is in knowing that what you do matters, including doing nothing!"

— Dr. Sylvia Earle (Mission Blue)

Following are several organizations you might consider, although the list is in no way exhaustive. Each organization is followed by the location(s) where they operate and a statement from the respective website:

Land/Forest Conservation

International Tree Foundation
> www.internationaltreefoundation.org

Operating: around the world with a particular focus on Africa and the U.K.

> *We work every day to plant and grow trees, restore and conserve forests and strengthen community and ecosystem resilience. We believe in transformational tree planting, because when tree planting is done right it changes landscapes, communities, and livelihoods.*

Nature Conservancy
> www.nature.org

Operating in: U.S., Africa, Asia Pacific, Canada, Caribbean, Europe, India, Latin America

The Nature Conservancy is a global environmental non-profit working to create a world where people and nature can thrive.

One Tree Planted

www.onetreeplanted.org

Planting in: 47+ countries in North America, Latin America, Africa, Asia, Europe and the Pacific

We want to make it simple for anyone to help the environment by planting trees. Together we can restore forests, create habitat for biodiversity, and make a positive social impact around the world. We plant one tree with every dollar donated.

Rainforest Action Network

www.ran.org

Operating: Globally

Rainforest Action Network preserves forests, protects the climate and upholds human rights by challenging corporate power and systemic injustice through frontline partnerships and strategic campaigns.

Rainforest Alliance

www.rainforest-alliance.org

Operating in: 70 countries

The Rainforest Alliance is creating a more sustainable world by using social and market forces to protect nature and improve the lives of farmers and forest communities. To achieve our mission, we partner with diverse allies around the world to drive positive change across global supply chains and in many of our most critically important natural landscapes.

Trees help clean the air we breathe, filter the water we drink, and provide habitat to over 80% of the world's terrestrial biodiversity. Forests provide jobs to over 1.6 billion people, absorb harmful carbon from the atmosphere, and are key ingredients in 25% of all medicines.

- One Tree Planted

Wildlife

Defenders of Wildlife
www.defenders.org

Operating in: The U.S.

Defenders of Wildlife works on the ground, in the courts, and on Capitol Hill to protect and restore imperiled wildlife and habitats across North America. Together, we can ensure a future for the wildlife and wild places we all love.

Endangered Species International
https://www.endangeredspeciesinternational.org/

Operating: Globally

Endangered Species International is strongly committed to reversing the trend of human-induced species extinction, saving endangered animals, and preserving wild places!

International Union for Conservation of Nature
www.iucn.org

Operating in: Asia, Eastern and Southern Africa, Eastern Europe and Central Asia, Europe, Mediterranean, Mexico, Central America, the Caribbean, North America, Oceania, South America, West and Central Africa, West Asia

> *The International Union for Conservation of Nature (IUCN) is a membership Union uniquely composed of both government and civil society organizations. By harnessing the experience, resources and reach of its more than 1,400 Member organizations and the input of some 15,000 experts, IUCN is the global authority on the status of the natural world and the measures needed to safeguard it.*

Jane Goodall Institute

www.janegoodall.org

Operating on: Every continent except Antarctica

> *The Jane Goodall Institute promotes understanding and protection of great apes and their habitat and builds on the legacy of Dr. Jane Goodall, our founder, to inspire individual action by young people of all ages to help animals, other people and to protect the world we all share.*

Pollinator Partnership

https://www.pollinator.org/

Operating: across North America and globally

> *Pollinator Partnership's mission is to promote the health of pollinators, critical to food and ecosystems, through conservation, education, and research.*

Save Our Monarchs

www.saveourmonarchs.org

Operating in: The U.S., Mexico, and Canada

We want to promote the recovery of the monarch population now. One milkweed at a time. The Save Our Monarchs Foundation is solely dedicated to saving the monarch butterfly by planting more milkweed.

World Conservation Society
www.wcs.org

Operating in: The Americas, Africa, Asia, and Oceania

WCS's goal is to conserve the world's largest wild places in 14 priority regions, home to more than 50% of the world's biodiversity.

World Wildlife Fund
www.worldwildlife.org

Operating on: Every continent

WWF works to sustain the natural world for the benefit of people and wildlife, collaborating with partners from local to global levels in nearly 100 countries.

More than ten million species remain to be discovered in the world; most of them highly threatened since they are located within regions of great habitat destruction. Amongst the 46,000 species assessed, more 17,000 are likely to become extinct in the very near future if no aggressive actions are taken.

– Endangered Species International

Ocean

Coral Reef Alliance

<u>www.coral.org</u>

Operating in: Hawaiʻi and the Mesoamerican Region (MAR)

We work at local, regional, and global levels to keep coral reefs healthy, so they can adapt to climate change and survive for generations to come. As one of the largest global NGOs focused exclusively on protecting coral reefs, the Coral Reef Alliance (CORAL) has used cutting-edge science and community engagement for nearly 30 years to reduce direct threats to reefs and to promote scalable and effective solutions for their protection.

Mission Blue

<u>www.mission-blue.org</u>

Operating: Globally

Mission Blue inspires action to explore and protect the ocean. Led by legendary oceanographer Dr. Sylvia Earle, Mission Blue is uniting a global coalition to inspire an upwelling of public awareness, access and support for a worldwide network of marine protected areas – Hope Spots.

Ocean Conservancy

<u>www.oceanconservancy.org</u>

Operating: From the Arctic to the Gulf of Mexico

Ocean Conservancy is working with you to protect the ocean from today's greatest global challenges. Together, we create evidence-based solutions for a healthy ocean and the wildlife and communities that depend on it.

Ocean Defenders Alliance

<u>www.oceandefenders.org</u>

Operating in: California and Hawai'i

Ocean Defenders Alliance works to clean and protect marine ecosystems through documentation, education, and meaningful action. Working with affected communities, we focus primarily on the reduction and removal of man-made debris which poses serious threats to ocean wildlife and habitats.

Ocean Voyages Institute
www.oceanvoyagesinstitute.org

Operating in: The U.S. and the North Pacific Ocean (the Great Garbage Patch)

Ocean Voyages Institute (OVI) is a 501(c)3 non-profit organization founded in 1979 by a group of international sailors, educators, and conservationists with a mission of teaching maritime arts and sciences and preserving the world's oceans.

"It is clear, now is the time, our global ocean is at a crucial crossroads. Our ocean cannot be our toxic waste dump. The oceans are the blue heart of our planet. For a healthy earth we must give our ocean ecosystem a chance to recover."

— Mary Crowley (Ocean Voyages Institute)

Employees

I will go into the importance of your employees in greater depth in Chapter 5, Employee Engagement, but let me touch on it briefly here. Your employees will be one of your greatest tools and assets in establishing and running your sustainability program, and by default, helping the environment. You can create the best sustainability program in the world, but without staff support, it may barely get off the ground. Conversely, you can put a rather basic sustainability program in place, and with the energy, enthusiasm, and contributions of your employees, you can make a big impact on your goals and the health of the environment. Do not underestimate the value and power of your employees.

Chapter Takeaways

According to the Environmental Protection Agency (EPA), in 2018, about 146.1 million tons of waste were landfilled in the United States alone, rather than being reused, recycled, repurposed, composted, or upcycled.

Air pollution contributes to 11.65% of deaths globally.

Ocean acidification is literally causing a sea change that is threatening the fundamental chemical balance of ocean and coastal waters from pole to pole.

Methane is the primary contributor to the formation of ground-level ozone, a hazardous air pollutant and greenhouse gas, exposure to which causes 1 million premature deaths every year. Methane is also a powerful greenhouse gas. Over a 20-year period, it is 80 times more potent at warming than carbon dioxide.

Trees help clean the air we breathe, filter the water we drink, and provide habitat to over 80 percent of the world's terrestrial biodiversity.

Your employees will be one of your greatest tools and assets in establishing and running your sustainability program, and by default, helping the environment. Do not underestimate the value and power of your employees.

Chapter 2

Create Your Mission Statement, Goals, and Procedures

Why have a sustainability program?

To begin, we need to discuss the reasons for and benefits of implementing a sustainability program, which I touched on in the introduction. As mentioned previously, the most obvious is: it is the right thing to do! Many of us know this at a gut level, if not an intellectual one. According to numerous scientific studies and reports, the environment is in peril, and everything each of us does has an impact, either negative or positive. We should each strive, individually and as organizations, to make as much of a positive impact as possible.

> "Protecting our environment is the foundation for sustaining our planet, community and economy. Our environment supports and houses our ecosystems, allowing them to grow and thrive. If we fail to protect our environment,

we will put the lives of humans, animals, plants and more at risk." – InspireCleanEnergy.com

The next most obvious reason for implementing a sustainability program is public perception, which directly ties to the fiscal health and viability of your business. Increasingly customers, vendors, and investors are asking about, if not demanding, corporate sustainability measures. You will see this in investor or customer questionnaires, in their own corporate sustainability goals and commitments, and in their general questions. This will only continue and increase in the foreseeable future. When customers or investors have a choice between two essentially equal companies, and one has its sustainability program in place while the other does not, they will almost certainly choose the one with its sustainability measures established. More and more, the public is looking to company websites to find their level of commitment to the environment. You do not want to get left behind.

> *"The demands of private customers are growing, just like those of institutional investors. The professionals, in particular, increasingly regard a lack of sustainability as a risk factor, because deficits in environmental protection, social issues and governance increase the danger of severe damage to reputation. In addition, politicians are exerting pressure through increasingly strict regulatory requirements."* – Frank Klein, Managing Director of the DWS's Global Client Group

Beyond customers and investors asking about corporate sustainability measures, this may soon be a requirement for publicly traded companies. At the time of this writing, the Securities and Exchange Commission (SEC) recently put out their proposed rules to enhance and standardize climate-related disclosures for investors. According to the SEC website:

Washington D.C., March 21, 2022 —

The Securities and Exchange Commission today proposed rule changes that would require registrants to include certain climate-related disclosures in their registration statements and periodic reports, including information about climate-related risks that are reasonably likely to have a material impact on their business, results of operations, or financial condition, and certain climate-related financial statement metrics in a note to their audited financial statements. The required information about climate-related risks also would include disclosure of a registrant's greenhouse gas emissions, which have become a commonly used metric to assess a registrant's exposure to such risks...

...The proposed rule changes would require a registrant to disclose information about (1) the registrant's governance of climate-related risks and relevant risk management processes; (2) how any climate-related risks identified by the registrant have had or are likely to have a material impact on its business and consolidated financial statements, which may manifest over the short-, medium-, or long-term; (3) how any identified climate-related risks have affected or are likely to affect the registrant's strategy, business model, and outlook; and (4) the impact of climate-related events (severe weather events and other natural conditions) and transition activities on the line items of a registrant's consolidated financial statements, as well as on the financial estimates and assumptions used in the financial statements.

While this is not yet official, these SEC changes may soon be adopted. And while they would currently only apply to publicly traded companies, if these go through, then the change is in the wind. This level of transparency will likely be expected in the future for all companies, so it behooves you to get ahead of that. It's better to be ahead of the game than to play catch-up later. And it certainly translates well to public opinion.

Before I move on from public perception, I want to address municipalities. I mentioned in the previous paragraph that customers, vendors, and investors are asking about, if not demanding, corporate sustainability measures. If you are a municipality, then it will be your stakeholders and residents who will demand sustainability policies and ordinances, including the business owners within your jurisdiction. You will no doubt see this on social media, as well as hear about it at your public commission or council meetings. This will only continue and increase in the foreseeable future. Unlike investors who have a choice between two essentially equal companies, residents do not typically have the luxury of choosing between two cities if they are already an established resident of one. However, if a potential resident is looking to move to the area, they may have options for which city they choose to reside in. The same is true for new businesses, which may choose to locate in the more sustainable city when considering new locations. And almost certainly, developers will exercise this choice as well (though there are many factors that go into developer choices, such as the permitting process and fees, the development appetite of the commission, the land value of the area, etc.).

> "*The notion of sustainable cities usually conjures environmental themes, but sustainable urban design's greatest impact could be on economic performance. By creating improved quality of life conditions for residents, sustainable cities simultaneously lay the foundation for wide-ranging economic benefits.*" – Hallie Kennan & Chris Busch, GreenBiz.com

Another big benefit to implementing your sustainability program, which I mentioned in the introduction, is attracting and retaining employees. Your attention to the environment will also make you more attractive to potential employees. You might be surprised how important this is. According to a report by PWC titled "The future of work: A journey to 2022", 65 percent of people in the U.S., Germany,

India, China, and the U.K. want to work for an organization with a strong social conscience. According to the online magazine *Worklife,* new research (as of 2021) from global recruitment firm Robert Walters indicates that 34 percent of U.K. office workers would refuse a job offer if a company's environmental, sustainability, or climate control values do not align with their own. In the U.S., the figure is even higher: 41 percent. France and Chile (both at 53 percent) top the list, closely followed by Switzerland (52 percent). This will only increase over time. I have found this to be anecdotally true in my own experience, as well.

I have received countless comments from staff about how happy they were to see what the company was doing for the environment, how pleased they were with the direction the company was going in terms of sustainability, or how much it meant to them that our senior executives cared about the environment (and routinely talked about it at the daily all-staff meetings). I have also heard from new employees that our (sustainability) department was one of the reasons they applied to work for the company! None of them had applied for a position in the sustainability department, it was just that important to them to work for a company that took sustainability seriously. To quote one such employee:

[I] really love that [our company] is taking sustainability so seriously!
– S.B. 3/14/22

I have talked a lot about public perception in this section, and will also mention marketing and PR in a future chapter. Obviously, a part of shaping public perception is sharing what you are doing. To that end, you will see that I have shared various examples of LinkedIn articles throughout this book where applicable, based on actual articles I have written. I have added these to serve as an example of one easy, free way to make your good works known.

Make Sure You Have Buy-in from the Top

Before you go any further, you need to make sure you have buy-in from your executives. I cannot stress this enough; for your sustainability program to be successful, you absolutely must have buy-in from the top. A very close second to having buy-in from the top is having buy-in from your employees, which I will discuss in Chapter 5, Employee Engagement.

I mentioned in the introduction that if you are just simply trying to check a box, then this book isn't for you. Along those same lines, if your leaders are only trying to check that box, then your sustainability program really will never get off the ground. If your leaders do not support you, then your path will be frustratingly bumpy, at best. So make sure that they support you, the mission statement that you create, and the goals that you establish. Make sure that it is in line with what they want to accomplish. You may, yourself, be "those executives", and if that's the case, then this is an easy first step. If you are not one of the C-suite executives (or the business owner, or commissioner, etc), then you may need to sit down with them, or you may need to draft your mission statement and goals and then provide it to them. Let them tell you if this is the direction they want to go, and if not, have them provide feedback. Then once they confirm, make sure they are committed.

If you don't initially have buy-in from your leaders, then you need to foster this. The easiest way is through education. The best approach is typically *not* to hammer it in or to shame your executives, but to show them the facts, and let them get there on their own. So educate your leaders on all the reasons mentioned in the section above, "Why have a Sustainability Program". You can do this in a group meeting, in one-on-ones, or in written form. One pretty effective way is to put together a PowerPoint that you present to them, either in a group or individually. I believe once they see the value in implementing a sustainability program, they will embrace it.

Establish your Mission Statement

I suggest that you start your sustainability journey by creating your mission statement. This does not have to be your first step, but I find that it makes it easier to outline the rest of your program. Once you know what you are trying to achieve, then you understand the steps that you need to take to get there. The key to creating your mission statement is that it rings true for your group. Be certain it makes sense for your company, and that it is both approved and embraced by the very top of your organization.

Once you have established that you have buy-in, and more importantly, support from the top, then it is time to check in with your company or organization. This is where you explore:

- What is your organization's culture?

- What is important to your company?

- What does your company produce?

- Or what services does it provide?

All of these things will help you to craft your mission statement. If your company is already established, then much of this information can come from your existing overall company mission statement. Check your website for guidance on your company culture. You will likely get direction from your executives on this as well, but you can also weigh in with employees on this. You can get a random sampling by simply asking people. Or put out a survey.

Following are a couple of simple, straightforward examples of mission statements that I pulled from the Green Business Bureau article titled, "Sustainability Statements: How To Write One That Resonates with Employees and Customers."

- *We are committed to a sustainable future and to improving the social, economic and environmental well-being of the community.*

- *Our goal is to improve the environment in our community by working with area businesses, community leaders and our neighbors to create a clean and safe place to live and work.*

Establish Your Goals

Next, it is time to establish your goals. Just what goals do you have?

- Are they energy-related goals? (Example: net zero carbon emissions by a certain date)

- Are they waste management goals? (Example: ___% diversion rate from landfill)

- Do you have a goal for your product? (Example: ___% recycled content)

- Is your company philanthropic? (Example: supporting worthy environmental organizations)

These are the things that you have to question. You want this mission statement and these goals to reflect your established organization and your company culture. If you are a new company, then obviously, you do not have an established culture. But that makes it even easier. If you are a new organization, you get to decide from the very beginning what your goals are. And a lot of times, that's easier because you're not having to implement a sustainability culture into your existing culture. The two grow together as one organizational culture.

Make Your Commitments

Finally, you need to make the commitments associated with your goals. Consider committing to a zero waste goal (more on that in Chapter 4, Measure Your Carbon Footprint). If you have a goal to produce net zero carbon emissions by a certain time, then make that commitment. You can make that commitment through an organization like The Climate Pledge, or something similar. Or it can be a commitment that you simply establish yourself and broadcast to your customers, your employees, your vendors, your residents, or all of the above. You can do this by putting it in your promotional materials, on your website, or on social media; the bottom line is, commit to it and then stick to it.

You also do not want to "greenwash", so make sure that what you are stating is accurate. Greenwashing is essentially when a company makes an unsubstantiated claim to mislead customers or investors into believing that a company's products, processes, or services are environmentally friendly when they, in fact, are not. Or they are less environmentally friendly than stated. Greenwashing also includes making statements about sustainability achievements that cannot be verified. Be sure you can achieve what you have committed to and be sure that you are doing what you claim you are doing. And if, for some reason, you find you are not able to achieve what you committed to, then be transparent about that as well.

I want to emphasize here that the sustainability message really needs to come from the top. Your employees will know if this is just "lip service", or if your leaders do not really have their heart in the program. Conversely, knowing that your executives are committed to your initiatives will absolutely matter to your employees. If your employees believe it matters to the top, they will naturally want to be a part of that, and will contribute to and forward the cause. I will share a comment from one employee to show how true this is. The comment was made in response to something one of the senior executives said at one of the all-staff meetings.

How cool to see [our senior executive] talking about sustainability with such passion! – M.M. 3/18/22

Judgment Free Zone

One piece of advice that I want to offer here, and I will likely mention elsewhere, is to realize that everyone is at a different place in the sustainability game, if you will. And I mentioned this in the introduction as well. You need to be sure that you are creating a judgment-free zone (I borrowed this concept from Graham Hill and his "Carbonauts" course that I will mention in Chapter 6, Employee Training). So, many of us recognize that being sustainable or protecting the environment is just the right thing to do. But not everyone does. Some people really do not believe that the environment needs protection, for whatever reason. So allow them the space to feel that way. Conversely, some folks feel it is the most important thing that we have to do, and it's wholly their passion and their main life goal. And that's beautiful, but not everyone is there. And then some people are just learning; they may know very little about sustainability, and have never thought much about it. Or maybe they know the term and they know that they want to protect the environment, but they have no idea how to do it. Make space for every single one of those people.

Really establish a judgment-free zone. For those people who do not believe that protecting the environment is important, as long as you give them the space to believe that, then they most likely will not feel compelled to resist your efforts. If you make them "wrong", then they will fight you every step of the way to be "right". Alienating a portion of your employees will never get you anywhere. Not anywhere good, anyway. For those employees, you can let them know the *other* reasons that you are establishing the sustainability program, aside from the importance of protecting the environment. Reasons such as to remain relevant and competitive in your field, or to meet SEC requirements. For those people who are just learning, if it is a judgment-free zone, then you take away the embarrassment. And for those people who are completely passionate about it, you allow them to be as passionate as they want to be and they won't feel self-conscious about it. Even better, get them engaged, have them lead the green team, or use them as a sounding board. Really, this is a good approach for anything you do. Create a judgment-free zone in anything you do, but particularly in this aspect where you are creating your sustainability program.

Sustainability Procedures

Ok, so now you have established your mission statement and goals, you have made your commitments, and you understand why having a sustainability program is important. So just what *is* that program? What procedures will you put in place? The rest of this book will touch on different ideas and procedures for you to consider. Some obvious and important aspects of your business are waste management, establishing a way to measure your carbon footprint, employee engagement, employee training, marketing, green facilities, and green products. So important are these, in fact, that I have dedicated a chapter to each one. I will try to pepper examples of these various procedures throughout the book.

As you are going through this exercise, I want to offer you a word of caution: beware of your blind spots. I will use a personal example to make my point. When I moved from municipal government to the corporate world, the planet was knee-deep in COVID lockdowns, and the majority of our staff was working remotely. As a result, we held our annual convention virtually. The following year, we held our convention in person. This was cause for celebration for not only our staff but also for our customers and tech fans. The ramifications of this did not occur to me until the conventions team was very far along in the planning stage. Because we had been virtual during my initial year, when I was putting into place our procedures, I had a blind spot on the convention once it went back to being in person again.

Thankfully, our conventions team was already quite savvy and forward-thinking. They put into place such things as converting to an electronic app for the convention, instead of producing brochures or printed materials. They selected our preferred 100 percent recycled t-shirts, without receiving a prompt from me. The swag they produced was reusable and was "offered" to attendees, rather than given to them automatically. Once the convention was over, I met with the person in charge of conventions and we worked out several more sustainable measures to put into place the following year. One such measure was to repurpose the pole wraps from the convention into bags to be handed out to attendees the following year (three cheers for reusable, repurposed swag!). I admit later on in the employee engagement section of this book that "many of my best ideas aren't mine". I need to profess that here as well. Most of the recommendations I made to the director of conventions were based on suggestions I received from another employee who attended conventions regularly; she was a treasure trove of inspired sustainable improvements and solutions.

So again, as you go through this exercise, take a look around. Endeavor to analyze *all* aspects of your business. Look for blind spots. Look at your office supplies, your break room supplies, your shipping procedures. Look at your energy usage, then look for ways to reduce this. Can you take advantage of natural light, or install motion sensors? Put monitors and printers into sleep mode? Take a look at your swag and gifts – are they reusable? Sustainably sourced? Truly useful? Look at your marketing materials – do they need to be physical, or can they be made virtual? If you produce products, look at your packaging and shipping materials; are you using the most economical size, the most environmentally friendly materials, etc? All of this will help you create a more holistic, comprehensive, and ultimately more successful sustainability program.

Depending on the size of your organization, you may want to codify your procedures by way of a sustainability policy, a sustainability master or strategic plan, or both. These can be as simple or as complex as you like. I am a fan of sweet and simple because I think the simpler a policy is, the easier it is to follow. If you decide to go in this direction, I would suggest you start by creating a policy and then see from there if you think there is a need for a full plan. Following is a super simple example of a sustainability policy from Press8 Telecom:

> ABC Company recognizes that businesses can have a negative impact on the environment. We are committed, and enjoy finding ways in which we can reduce the impact of our work both in the office and when work takes us away from the office.
>
> It is our policy to:
>
> • Recycle as much waste material as possible.
>
> • Avoid the use of paper wherever possible. For example, sending invoices and quotes via email as PDF files.
>
> • Recycling equipment that is no longer of use to the company. For example, giving away items such as computers and printers that we no longer use.

- Keep energy usage low. For example, making use of low energy light bulbs throughout and ensuring that computers are shut down after work.

- Reuse waste paper (from the printer) where possible, making use of the blank side for notes, etc.

- Purchase products made with recycled paper. For example, paper towels, printer paper.

- Purchase products with a lower environmental impact. For example environmentally safe soaps and detergents.

- Use low impact transport for travel to and from work and travel for business. For example, we use public transport to attend meetings and offer a Cycle Scheme to encourage staff to cycle to work or to carpool.

- Avoid unnecessary travel by making use of instant messaging, video and audio conferencing, telephone, and email.

As I will caution throughout this book, be sure that your policy is specific to your company. For example, if your employees do not travel, then there is no need to touch on that. Once you have finalized your policy and have your necessary approvals, make sure to share it with staff. Make it accessible to your employees and include it in your onboarding or new hire training materials. There is no point in having a lovely policy if no one is following it, or even aware of it.

We adopted beehives for our company anniversary!

August 15th is National Honey Bee Day! According to the Greenpeace website, honey bees — wild and domestic — perform about 80 percent of all pollination worldwide. A single bee colony can pollinate 300 million flowers each day. Grains are primarily pollinated by the wind, but fruits, nuts, and vegetables are pollinated by bees. Seventy out of the top 100 human food crops — which supply about 90 percent of the world's nutrition — are pollinated by bees. And it's not just about food. According to PlanetBee, pollinators help plants survive, and plants:

> Produce one-third of our food supply by giving us countless fruits, vegetables, and nuts

Provide half of the world's oils, fibers (such as the cotton used to make clothes), and other raw materials

Are used to create many medicines

Provide food and cover for wildlife

Keep waterways clean

Prevent soil erosion

Produce the oxygen we breathe

Absorb CO_2, counteracting global climate change

What better way to celebrate National Honey Bee Day, than by starting a beehive? How about by starting (__#) beehives? That's right, for our #th anniversary, ABC Company made a donation through the Pinellas Beekeepers Association (PBA) to establish and maintain __# full honey bee hives throughout the season. Each mature hive, or colony, will house approximately 20,000 - 35,000 honey bees. That means ABC's donation is ultimately adding between 220,000 and 385,000 bees to the planet! Said another way, our bees will pollinate about *3.3 billion* flowers a day (yes, 3,300,000,000).

The purpose of the PBA is to support the Florida State Beekeepers Association (FSBA); develop and promote Florida best management practices and other practical beekeeping methods; educate members and the general public to promote the use of honey, beehive products, and beekeeping; act in the interest of beekeepers protecting and carrying on beekeeping affairs; act as a medium for, and an aid in, cooperative and mutual beekeeping methods; and encourage PBA members to act as mentors and be available to help others.

Between pesticides, loss of habitat, pollution, climate change, and parasites, bees can use all the help they can get. And the good news is, humans are able to provide that help.

If you're an individual interested in learning to keep bees, check out PBA (if you're local), or find a beekeeper's association in your area.

If your company is interested in sponsoring hives or making a donation (and I hope it is!), please contact the PBA (https://pinellas-beekeepers.buzz/corporate-sponsorships/) or look for a beekeeper's association in your area.

How will you commemorate National Honey Bee Day?

 42   5 shares

 Like   Comment   Share   Send

Be the first to comment on this

Chapter Takeaways

The most obvious reason to create a sustainability program is because it is the right thing to do!

Protecting our environment is the foundation for sustaining our planet, community, and economy. Our environment supports and houses our ecosystems, allowing them to grow and thrive. If we fail to protect our environment, we will put the lives of humans, animals, plants, and more at risk.

The next most obvious reason for implementing a sustainability program is public perception, which directly ties to the fiscal health and viability of your business. Increasingly, customers, vendors, and investors are asking about, if not demanding, corporate sustainability measures.

Your attention to the environment will also make you more attractive to potential employees.

Make sure you have buy-in from your executives. I cannot stress this enough; for your sustainability program to be successful, you absolutely must have buy-in from the top.

I suggest that you start your sustainability journey by creating your mission statement. Next, establish your goals. Finally, you need to make the commitments associated with those goals.

One piece of advice is to be sure that you are creating a judgment-free zone.

Throughout the process of establishing your sustainability program, stay aware of your blind spots.

Chapter 3

Waste Management

O ne of the largest aspects of a sustainability program that you will likely face is your waste management plan. It seems simple, right? You throw your trash in the trash can. That's your waste management plan. But there is a lot more to it than that. Or there should be a lot more to it than that. But again, this is a judgment-free zone. So I won't pressure you, but I will strongly suggest that you pursue this. My best suggestion for setting up your own waste reduction program is to look into zero waste training. There are a few different certification programs out there. One is the TRUE (Total Resource Use and Efficiency) certification program. Another option is ZWIA (Zero Waste International Alliance) training. I believe there are other organizations as well. I'm not saying you need to certify your program, but I am letting you know that there is a wealth of information out there.

Zero Waste Plan

I, personally, became a certified TRUE Advisor. I found the program invaluable; it is hands down why I was able to create such a successful waste management program on my first attempt. The training provided so many ideas that I had not considered; there were a lot of aspects to zero waste management that just had not occurred to me. And I had been in sustainability for quite a long time at that point. For instance, I did not realize what I could count and what I could not count toward zero waste. Hint, there is a lot more you can count than you probably realize. That is where taking advantage of one of these zero waste training programs will really come in handy for you as you are creating that Zero Waste Plan.

Again, it is easiest if you have a bit of a template and that is what I received from the TRUE Advisor training and certification. A meaningful plan will cover many, if not all, of the following categories:

- Redesign

- Reduce

- Reuse

- Compost (Re-earth)

- Recycle

- Zero Waste Reporting

- Diversion from Landfill, Incineration (WTE), and Environment

- Zero Waste Purchasing

- Leadership

- Training

- Zero Waste Analysis

- Upstream Management

- Hazardous Waste Prevention

- Closed Loop System

- Innovation

If this comprehensive list makes your head swim, I encourage you to look into training. Once you get an understanding of the concept and approach, this will all make sense. And you will likely find many more ways to reduce waste than you thought possible. Training will help in figuring out how you get to whatever goal you set for your waste reduction, and I do recommend setting a zero waste goal or target. In my initial Zero Waste Plan, we started with a goal of an 80% diversion rate from landfill. The zero waste industry recommends a 90% diversion rate from landfill. That is ambitious, and it is difficult, but it is also doable. The way you get there is by getting very creative. So again, look at a zero waste training management program to obtain information and guidance.

Initiating the Zero Waste Program

Next, I will outline some of the ways that we got to our goals, and you can use these suggestions or not. The first thing I did was to write our company's Zero Waste Plan, comprising an introduction and 12 sections. Through writing the plan, I thoroughly explored the existing conditions and where we wanted to get. This exercise will be eye-opening and invaluable to your organization. Following are some examples of changes you may make, or procedures you may implement:

- Eliminate disposable items for your break room(s), such as paper cups, plates, etc

- Replace disposable items with durable dishes, cups, and utensils

- Recycle e-waste (broken, used, or obsolete electronics) rather than sending to landfill

- Donate old furniture or equipment, rather than sending to the dump (consider schools, non-profit organizations, Habitat for Humanity, etc)

- Recycle metal furniture and equipment (this could create a revenue stream, rather than hauling expenses)

You may find many such opportunities as you go through the exercise of writing and implementing your plan.

Next, you need to map out how you plan to collect your metrics. We used Diversion, a weight-based measurement, which, according to David Rachelson, is a well-respected and often-used measurement for zero waste credentialing. Diversion refers to the amount of waste material diverted from the landfill. In other words, it's the amount of waste sorted for recycling, whether that's headed to a curbside recycling facility or another non-landfill destination. Rachelson explains that diversion is an important benchmark for tracking performance over time, and that it is still the single best tool to measure recycling. Diversion rates offer a highly accurate standard by which to track improvements, or even setbacks, on the journey to waste reduction and less landfill dependence. Having said that, using weight for your metrics is not perfect. For example, comparing a collection of plastic bags to several metal cabinets, both of which are being recycled, hardly seems, well, comparable. But weight is the simplest way to measure, and it keeps everything standard, so it is typically how companies track their waste metrics.

Once you have established whether you are measuring your materials by weight or volume, or some other form of measurement, you should establish your baseline. You will need to find what your current diversion rate is so that you have a benchmark for your metrics against which you can measure your organization's improvements. I won't go into details here, because again, you can find all of that in any zero-waste training. Once you have your baseline, set a goal for your new diversion rate, and then set a schedule for how often you will re-measure. This could be monthly, quarterly, twice a year, or annually. Put it on your calendar to make sure it gets done and make sure that you measure everything!

Expanded Employee Recycling

I would say probably the most successful action that we took was the expanded employee recycling program that we established. And again, this is going to look different in every region, at least from state to state, possibly from city to city, and certainly from country to country. Where our company headquarters is located, there are not a whole lot of recycling resources. There is a very limited number of items that we can recycle at our curbside pickup and we do not have at this writing an industrial composting option.

So we got creative with our expanded recycling program. One of the first things we did was establish a grassroots composting program. That meant first finding out what compostable items we had. We did not want individual employees having to collect leftover lunches and whatnot, so that is not what we targeted with our grassroots composting program. We targeted things like coffee grounds. At our corporate headquarters, we had several break rooms, and every day each of those break rooms produced a substantial amount of coffee grounds. The company offered free snacks and treats in the break rooms as well, and some of those treats were organic fruits and veggies. So we were able to compost the fruits and vegetables that had become overripe, as well as the cuttings and scraps.

Once we established just what and how much we had to compost, I put out a post on our intranet. I let everyone know what we had to compost and asked anyone interested in composting to please let us know. I was obviously one of the first staff to compost, just to get it off the ground. We had about four or five employees who came and picked up compost as we had it available. So that was an easy way to take all of the coffee grounds and fruits and vegetables out of our waste stream.

Another thing we did was to establish an entire closet at our headquarters to collect other recyclables that were not picked up by our solid waste providers. Our solid waste providers only picked up paper, cardboard, plastic bottles, tetra paks, and cans. That leaves a lot in the waste stream! So I got creative, and just started searching for what recycling options were out there. I was thrilled to find that there are a lot of options available. We started by collecting personal e-waste (broken or used electronics), printer cartridges of all types, and reusable bags (there is a company in Chico, California, that recycles reusable bags!). Then someone asked about batteries, so we found a recycling resource so that we were able to recycle all types of batteries (single-use, rechargeable, large, small, etc.). Later, I discovered a program through TerraCycle and Bic that recycles office supplies such as glue sticks and pens for free. We also had bins in each of our break rooms to collect and recycle plastic bags on behalf of our staff. Bonus – the plastic bags are then converted into outdoor equipment such as park benches, win-win!

Expanded Recycling Program for Employees

(Photo credit: Artem Beliaikin)

Most of us know there is a lot more that we can recycle beyond the standard paper/cardboard, cans, and plastic. Unfortunately, many areas in the U.S., such as our region of Florida, only include these few items in their standard solid waste collection service. That's where ABC Company's expanded recycling program comes in.

There are several items we recycle in our headquarters as a courtesy to our staff and the planet. In addition to the usual suspects, we offer the following courtesy recycling for our local employees:

Plastic bags: We collect about 15 types of plastic bags and wrap and deliver these to a <u>NexTrex</u> drop-off location to be converted into park benches and outdoor equipment.

Reusable shopping bags: We collect used, ripped, or torn reusable bags, and ship these to a company called <u>ChicoBag</u>. They will distribute the usable ones to fixed and low-income families ready to start a reusable bag habit, or they will recycle them into new, useful products through partnerships with artists, crafters, and non-profit organizations.

Pens, glue sticks, etc: We recycle these through <u>TerraCycle</u>.

E-Waste (broken or used electronics): We collect over 20 types of e-waste, which we recycle through a local e-waste recycling company called <u>Urban e-Recycling</u>.

Batteries: We recycle single-use and rechargeable batteries with a couple of different companies, depending on the size of the battery.

In addition to these items that we recycle at our offices, there are even more recyclable items that often go overlooked, such as mattresses, styrofoam, shoes, and glasses. I encourage you to explore recycling resources in your area.

Green Purchasing Policy

Next, you want to work on your green purchasing policy, or as it's known in the zero waste industry, your environmentally preferred purchasing policy. According to the National Association of State Procurement Officials (NASPO), "Environmentally Preferable Purchasing (EPP) or Green Purchasing is generally defined as purchasing a product that has a lesser or reduced negative effect or increased positive effect on human health and the environment, when compared with competing products that serve the same purpose. Incorporating EPP in the procurement process considers raw materials acquisition, production, fabrication, manufacturing, packaging, distribution, reuse, operation, maintenance, and disposal of the product. This term includes sourcing recyclable products, recycled products, reusable products, and products that conserve energy or natural resources. EPP is used interchangeably to mean either environmentally preferable purchasing or an environmentally preferable product...Environmentally preferable products or Sustainable Products (SP) are generally defined as products and services that have a lesser or reduced effect on human health and the environment when compared to competing products or services that serve the same purpose. As buying and using sustainable products benefits the environment, improves efficiency, and often saves money, in recent years these practices have become an integral part of public procurement." I would also point out one nuance, which is that the

43

TRUE zero waste certification program calls this Environmentally Preferred (rather than preferable) Purchasing.

While an EPP is not required, I do strongly suggest putting one in place. This does not need to be in any way bureaucratic or overly formal. You want this to be a tool for your purchasing agent or your purchasing department. They should be able to use this as a guide to actually make their purchasing more sustainable. So you might want to include links to actual catalogs or names of products. If you do this, be sure to revisit your policy periodically to make sure the links and/or product recommendations are still relevant. You certainly want to make sure that you know what your company is buying. So if your company only buys paper and you write a purchasing policy that covers 1500 different items or categories, that is not going to be an appropriate policy, no one will read it, and it will not be meaningful. Just like everything else you do in your sustainability program, make sure that this policy is meaningful.

A mature leafy tree produces as much oxygen in a season as 10 people inhale in a year.

~ ThoughtCo.

Sample Environmentally Preferred Purchasing Policy (EPP)

Below is a sample EPP from Babson College. As you can see, the policy is simple and straightforward, and pertains to their business. There is no need to overthink or overcomplicate your policy. Design it to work for your specific organization.

**Green Purchasing Policy
Mission Statement**

Babson's Green Purchasing Policy demonstrates our commitment to environmental sustainability. By purchasing "Green" products, Babson will lead the way in playing a significant role in the development of environmental sustainability on campus and in the local community.

Goals

Babson will strive to balance environmental and fiscal responsibilities in making Green Purchasing decisions. We will promote the purchase of products with the highest percentage of recycled content available, provided that the products meet acceptable use and performance standards.

The Importance of Green Purchasing

Sustainable development involves using the Earth's natural resources (i.e. both renewable and non-renewable resources) to fulfill our present needs without affecting the needs of next generations. "Green Purchasing" is an important element to achieve sustainable development. Consequently, when one considers buying something, he/she should think about the adverse environmental impacts associated with the product during its full life-cycle.

However, environmentally preferable products are sometimes more expensive to purchase than alternative products. This circumstance can discourage green purchasing by consumers seeking lower costing products without significant environmental benefits. Nevertheless, buying "greener products" doesn't necessarily mean paying more, especially when other cost factors are considered.

It is important to recognize and appreciate that proper and effective green purchasing doesn't simply lead to environmental benefits, but also helps purchasers reduce full life-cycle costs and thus save money. For practitioners, another significant benefit of green purchasing is the major contribution its adoption and application can make to the establishment and demonstration of a broader overall Corporate Social Responsibility (CSR) strategy and image.

Green Purchasing

Green Purchasing is the practice of procuring goods and services that cause less harm to the environment and the living beings that depend upon it for survival. Green Products are those manufactured with more environmentally friendly materials or which are produced with minimal impact to the environment.

Babson will strive to purchase materials that are:

- Durable, as opposed to single-use or disposable

- Non-toxic or minimally toxic, preferably biodegradable

- Highly energy-efficient

- Recyclable or safely disposable

- Made from raw materials obtained in an environmentally sound, sustainable manner

- Manufactured in an environmentally sound manner

- The cause of minimal or no environmental damage during normal use or maintenance

- Shipped with minimal packaging (consistent with care of the product), preferably made of recycled and/or recyclable materials

Products that meet the above criteria will be considered Green Products.

Procedures

Babson College is committed to minimizing the College's impact on the environment and reducing the College's dependence on non-renewable energy. This Committee is charged with establishing guidelines for the College's Sustainable Practices including: Green Building Design; Green Building Renovations; Climate Protection Practices; Clean Energy Standards; Sustainable Transportation Practices; Sustainable Operations; Recycling and Waste Management; and Environmentally Preferable Procurement.

When appropriate, Babson will include a clause in its bidding specifications that reads: "Babson is committed to buying products with recycled content or environmentally sustainable alternatives. Please offer any alternatives that you feel are available for this product and supply all relevant specific information about the product."

Any existing limitation within Babson's Policies and Procedures prohibiting or restricting the purchase or use of recycled product shall be amended to encourage the purchase and use of recycled products to conform to this policy.

Initiatives

5 Gallon Bottled Water

Summer of 2010 Babson College began installing filtered water coolers to the Administrative offices, switching from 5 gallon plastic bottles to a filtration system, using our own town water. Babson College is cutting down on emissions caused by water delivery trucks.

Copy Paper

Babson College's preference is to purchase copy paper with at least 30 percent recycled content. Babson College has been using 30 percent recycled color copy paper for many years. Babson College now prints day-to-day e-mails, reports, forms and other miscellaneous items doubled sided.

Office Supplies/Letterhead/Business Card Stock

In support of Babson's commitment to sustainability, the Purchasing Department, in partnership with Marketing Media and Staples, recently made the following changes in stationery available through Staples Advantage:

- • Replaced the paper used to print Babson's corporate identity suite of business cards, letterhead, and envelopes from a virgin stock to a locally milled FSC certified paper. The new letterhead is 30% post-consumer waste (PCW) (25% cotton by-products) and the business card stock is 100% PCW.

- • For quick access to recycled content of office products on Staples Advantage, search "recycled" once you enter the site. Look for the following icons:

"Ecoffice"

> This icon indicates an item that has one or more of the following attributes: Recycled, Comprehensive Procurement Guidelines, Environmentally Preferable Purchasing, Green Seal Certified or Environmentally Friendly.

Recycled

> Indicates an item that contains at least 10% Recycled Content.

Comprehensive Procurement Guidelines

> Indicates items that are part of EPA's continuing effort to promote the use of materials recovered from solid waste.

Environmentally Preferable Purchasing

> Indicates products that have a lesser or reduced effect on human health and the environment.

Green Seal Certification

> Indicates products that meet or exceed the Green Seal standards.

Environmentally Friendly

> Indicates an item that is environmentally preferable compared to similar items in the same category. Some of these products meet or exceed the Comprehensive Procurement Guidelines and/or Environmentally Preferable Purchasing Guidelines.

Mattresses

- Upholstery over springs is made up of shoddy fibers. (Shoddy fibers are recycled pre-consumer waste product.

- Steel is recycled.

- After the mattress's useful life, the polyester fire barrio can be recycled.

  Currently, Facilities is donating any mattress that can be reused. Mattresses that are not donated are recycled through IRN and they are burned for waste energy.

Copiers/Printers

  The college reaches out to the community to collect all printers, scanners and fax machines that are not being utilized.

Following is an even simpler example of a policy in the form of a statement from the non-profit organization, Endangered Species International:

At Endangered Species International, we do what we preach, no exceptions!

- We use 100% recycled, processed chlorine-free papers with soy-based ink.

- We generate our 100% carbon free electricity in the field from solar energy.

- While in the field in remote areas, we purify our water using SteriPEN with solar charging case (thanks to our partner SteriPEN). We also provide local communities in needs with safe drinking water using SteriPEN and solar energy.

- We use rechargeable batteries for our field equipment. Our batteries are recharged using solar battery chargers.

- We use minimal electricity consumption. No waste and overuse!

- We switch to a green energy supplier when available.

- We recycle all waste materials, including paper, cardboard, aluminum can, toner cartridges, and more.

- Most of our correspondences are via e-mail to reduce paper use.

- We set printers to print double-sided by default and print only when it is necessary.

- We buy locally.

- We avoid using air conditioning in hotels, and we favor places with natural ventilation when available.

- The use of regular plastic bags is not allowed in our conservation projects! Plastic bags, plastic bottle tops and polystyrene foam coffee cups are often found in the stomachs of dead sea lions, dolphins, sea turtles and others!

- When we need flagging for our projects, we only use environmentally safe plastic flagging that photodegrades after 6 months.

- We use rechargeable batteries for our field equipment. Our batteries are recharged using solar battery chargers. We use mostly eneloop batteries which are rechargeable and reusable

1000 times. Further, the batteries are 100% recyclable and we recycle them at www.rbrc.org

- Our website is powered by 100% wind energy.

Everybody working with us must get on board with all the above environmental policies.

The key is to remember to design your green purchasing policy, or your EPP to match your needs. If your company does a heavy amount of purchasing, then your policy may be several pages long. But if your purchasing is not terribly varied or complex, then you can likely write a succinct policy that is easy to read, easy to use, and easy to follow. The last thing you want to do is to write a long, overly wordy policy that will simply collect dust on the proverbial shelf.

Eco Swag

One important thing to keep in mind when putting together your green purchasing policy or EPP is to make sure that it covers swag or gifts. Outline what you would like to see in terms of swag. Again, this should be a useful tool or guide for your staff so that it is easy for them to make responsible choices. This could be swag for your staff – gifts, prizes, awards, etc. Or it could be swag for customers, existing or potential.

One key to creating eco swag is being sure that the items are durable and reusable, rather than disposable. Tumblers or mugs with your company logo on them are a great example of this. And it can tie into your overall sustainability program. For instance, if your break rooms or break areas currently have disposable cups, you need to get rid of these! And what better solution than to supply insulated tumblers to replace the coffee cups, and reusable water bottles to replace paper cups? Look for these in fun colors or designs and make sure the content/material of the cups, bottles, and tumblers is environmentally friendly and healthy (stainless steel rather than aluminum tumblers, and recycled, BPA-free plastic bottles).

Another important factor to eco swag is that it is environmentally friendly. For example, if you make t-shirts for your employees, look for ones that are locally made, or that are made of recycled materials, or that use environmentally friendly dyes, or ideally, all of the above! Look for gifts that are reusable, recyclable, and/or made from recycled materials. Make sure that they are able to be disposed of in an environmentally friendly manner once they've reached the end of their life or usefulness.

Finally, make sure your swag is useful. If you send cards to customers or employees, look for cards made from recycled paper, or from hemp, or consider seed paper cards. These are cards made from paper infused with seeds, which you can plant in the garden and grow flowers or herbs. Consider umbrellas, coffee mugs, or lunch boxes made from recycled materials. If yours is a tech company, consider branded thumb drives or cordless phone chargers made of bamboo. If yours is a gardening company, you could get branded flower pots or seed packets. You may be surprised to find the extensive variety of items that can be branded and the extent of eco choices out there.

Basically, look for the most responsibly sourced materials, made by the most environmentally responsible companies and vendors. This is becoming more and more of a demand, so most promotional product companies at this point have a pretty large array of environmentally friendly gifts and swag. Find these resources, research them, and then list them in your EPP.

Make Reusable Swag the Norm

Like many companies, ABC Company has set sustainability goals and targets. As an organization, ABC Company has committed to net zero carbon by 2040 and has an initial zero waste goal of an 80% diversion rate from landfill. So, how do we invite our employees to contribute to those goals?

One of those ways is by providing reusable swag. Looking for a fun gift for your employees? Make sure it is useful and reusable! One of our favorites is reusable cups and tumblers, and they have stood the test of time. Employees love to compare tumblers over time, and with their co-workers.

 42   5 shares

 Like   💬 Comment   ↱ Share   ✈ Send

Innovation

Innovation is where you get creative and start to think outside the box. This is going to be crucial if you have set any type of zero waste goals for your company. You will need to stretch and think in different ways about your waste. For example, when I started at one company, whenever they had furniture that they needed to get rid of, they would call a junk hauler to take it away, who charged the company a premium for the service. Once we put the Zero Waste Plan into place, we changed our operating basis. We looked for resources to donate to, such as local schools, Habitat for Humanity, etc. From then on, we donated our furniture, rather than sending it to the landfill. At one point, we had several (over 100, to be more precise) metal cabinets that we needed to dispose of. So we found a local recycler who recycled all sorts of metals. They ended up paying *us* a premium for the cabinets. So we essentially killed three birds with one stone:

- We no longer paid a fee to dispose of the cabinets,

- We no longer sent the cabinets to the landfill, *and*

- We actually made money by recycling them.

Donating anything your organization no longer needs is an excellent zero waste option. There are typically plenty of local non-profits where the goods go directly to those in need, rather than some of the larger "chain" non-profits where goods are rumored to be sorted, shipped, and sometimes disposed of rather than repurposed. If possible, choose local, reputable non-profits when deciding where to donate. For instance, if you have extra office supplies, furniture, or kitchen/break room supplies, see if there is a local homeless or women's shelter that could use your goods. For example, at one company, we held periodic catered lunches for our employees. Whenever there were untouched leftovers, we donated those to a local homeless shelter. We donated kitchen supplies to a local women's center. And our desk bins went to local public schools.

Another way to get innovative is to put your repurposing imagination to work. Let me give you another real-world example. Our company, at one point, had a huge banner hung on their 12-story headquarters. They also had a plane pull a banner around the city for an event. Those two banners were then put into storage once they were no longer used. By the time I started there, the banners had been in a storage closet for a couple of years. They knew they didn't want to send these to the landfill, but also didn't know what to do with them. So we got creative, and rather than throw them away, or continue to store them indefinitely, we put our thinking caps on. We decided to repurpose them into reusable shopping bags! We found a local seamstress who was able to do the job, and were able to make over 1,000 reusable bags, and saved nearly 350 pounds from going to the landfill. Each employee got a reusable bag, and essentially a little slice of our company history, in the form of a useful, lasting memento.

It's Time to Up Your Repurposing Game

Photo by Utopia By Cho on Unsplash

One of the many ways to take care of our environment is to follow the "Rs". Most people have probably heard about the "three Rs": Reduce, Reuse, and Recycle. However, the three Rs have been expanded to include a few more, so we now have: Reduce, Refuse, Reuse, Redesign, Repurpose, Re-earth (compost), and Recycle.

In this article, I discuss Repurposing, with a real-world example. In 20__, ABC Company hung a celebratory sign on one of our two office buildings and flew an airplane banner around the city.

In the spirit of taking extreme ownership of our environment, we took the sign and the banner, and rather than throwing them away, we are repurposing them into reusable shopping bags for each of our employees.

By doing so, we are diverting ___# pounds of trash from the landfill, which contributes towards our zero waste goals. At the same time, we are helping eliminate the use of plastic grocery bags by creating reusable ones. Not to mention each of our employees will get to own a little bit of ABC Company history. All while supporting a local small business. And that's how you repurpose.

Repurposing projects are not always obvious, but they are almost always worth it. At ABC Company, environmental responsibility is not just our company stance, it's our culture; it is who we are.

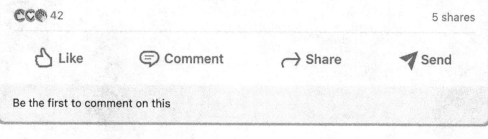

CC👍 42   5 shares

👍 Like   💬 Comment   ↱ Share   ✈ Send

Be the first to comment on this

Chapter Takeaways

One of the largest aspects of a sustainability program that you will likely face is your waste management plan.

Start by writing your zero waste plan and map out how you plan to collect your metrics.

One of your most successful actions may be establishing an expanded employee recycling program.

You will want to write your green purchasing policy, or as it's known in the zero waste industry, your environmentally preferred purchasing policy (EPP).

One important thing to keep in mind when putting together your green purchasing policy or EPP is that it covers swag or gifts.

Innovation is where you get creative and start to think outside the box. This is going to be crucial if you have set any type of zero waste goals for your company.

Chapter 4

Measure Your Carbon Footprint

When we talk about measuring your carbon footprint, we are talking about measuring the following greenhouse gasses per the Greenhouse Gas Protocol (GHGP):

The GHG Protocol Corporate Accounting and Reporting Standard provides requirements and guidance for companies and other organizations preparing a corporate-level GHG emissions inventory.

The standard covers the accounting and reporting of seven greenhouse gasses covered by the Kyoto Protocol:

- carbon dioxide (CO_2)

- methane (CH_4)

- nitrous oxide (N_2O)

- hydrofluorocarbons (HFCs)

- perfluorocarbons (PCFs)

- sulfur hexafluoride (SF6)

- nitrogen trifluoride (NF3)

It was updated in 2015 with the Scope 2 Guidance, which allows companies to credibly measure and report emissions from purchased or acquired electricity, steam, heat, and cooling.

-from the ghgprotocol.org website

Measuring your carbon footprint can seem a bit daunting. Ok let's be honest – it's daunting! Keep in mind that this is not a necessity unless you are a publicly traded company (at least at the time of this writing). And while measuring your carbon emissions is not yet *required* for public companies, it most likely will be required by the SEC very soon. Either way, if you have decided to tackle this for your business, I can provide some guidance. If you have an environmental science background, then this is probably right up your alley, and you may embrace doing the measuring on your own. If so, kudos to you! There are plenty of resources online explaining how to go about doing that. For the rest of us, using a consultant or third-party vendor may be the way to go.

Why Measure

So why measure? If you are a publicly traded company, then you are likely aware that investors are weighing ESG (environmental, social, and governance) considerations when making investment decisions. If they have the option of choosing between two companies which are fiscally sound, and one of them is measuring their carbon emissions (and has made reduction commitments, etc.), and one hasn't, they will most likely go with the company that is measuring its carbon footprint. And consumers and employees are also increasingly seeking additional engagement, transparency, and commitments on these issues. According to an article by Sam Harris on Ecoact.com, knowing your carbon footprint can also provide an initial climate risk and opportunities assessment by identifying emissions hotspots across your value chain. You can use the findings to inform your sustainability actions. You need to know your carbon footprint, the sources of your emissions, and the impact your footprint has on the environment before you can reduce it.

Short of doing your own measuring, I recommend partnering with a company that can work with you on this. Do your research; make sure they have ample experience and a good reputation. And make sure you get along with them, as you will be having a fair number of conversations and interactions with them. In order to establish your baselines, you will need to provide things like your office square footage, number of employees, power bill usages, etc. If you have onsite power generation (such as a furnace) you will provide that information. If you have multiple offices, you will provide this information for each one, including international offices. This is all for your Scope 1 and Scope 2 emissions. Let me pause here to provide some definitions:

- Scope 1 emissions are direct emissions from owned or controlled sources (such as a furnace).

- Scope 2 emissions are indirect emissions from the generation of purchased electricity, steam, heating, and cooling consumed by your company.

- Scope 3 emissions include all other indirect emissions that occur, such as purchased goods and services. This includes business travel, employee commuting, use of sold products, transportation and distribution (up- and downstream), investments, etc. We need to do a bit of a deep dive here, to give a clearer picture of Scope 3 emissions. Scope 3 emissions include the following categories:

- ◦ purchased goods and services

- ◦ capital goods

- ◦ fuel- and energy-related activities

- ◦ transportation and distribution

- ◦ waste generated in operations

- ◦ business travel

- ◦ employee commuting

- ◦ leased assets

- ◦ processing of sold products

- ◦ use of sold products

- ◦ end-of-life treatment of sold products

- ◦ franchises

- ◦ investments

In Harris' article on Ecoact.com, he explains that data collection for Scope 3 emissions involves multiple stakeholders and data sources, which makes them more challenging. However, Scope 3 emissions are important as they often account for a significant proportion of a company's carbon footprint—sometimes up to 90 percent. Scope 3 emissions are definitely the trickiest to track, and not everyone is measuring them at this point. At the time of this writing, Scope 3 collection is still a bit hazy. The practice has not been standardized, and different companies may collect and measure this data in different ways. By the time you read this book, measuring Scope 3 may or may not be the norm. But if you do intend to measure Scope

3, then for that reason alone, I recommend using a third party to measure your carbon footprint.

You may be asking, don't Scope 3 emissions get double counted? For instance, my Scope 3 emissions may be my supplier's Scope 1 or 2 emissions. Well, the answer is yes, there is a certain assumed amount of double counting. I like the way that BHP (Broken Hill Proprietary Company Limited) explains this in their 2018 prospectus:

> By definition, scope 3 emissions occur from sources owned or controlled by other entities in the value chain, and in certain cases, two or more companies may account for the same emissions within the scope 3 inventories they calculate. This type of double counting is an inherent characteristic of scope 3 accounting, and it is why scope 3 emissions should not be aggregated across companies to determine total emissions in a given sector or region. Double counting between companies is considered acceptable because it is recognized that each entity in the value chain has differing degrees of influence and different opportunities to reduce emissions, so allowing this form of double counting within scope 3 accounting facilitates the simultaneous action of multiple entities to contribute to the reduction of emissions.

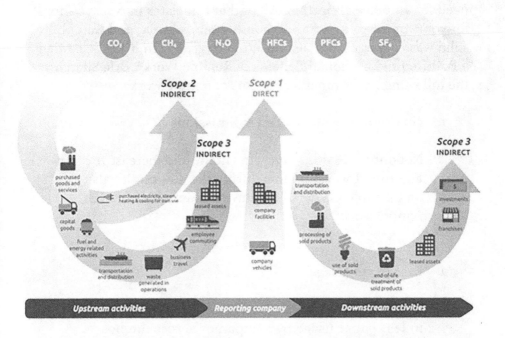

The three scopes of greenhouse gas emissions, taken from the Greenhouse Gas Protocol: https://ghgprotocol.org/

Reductions

Once you have completed your first greenhouse gas audit, you will have your carbon footprint baseline. Going forward, you will continue measuring this each year, with the goal of seeing a reduction year after year. Your baseline should be able to provide you with a picture of where your largest emissions are, providing you with where to target your reductions. Now it is time to get creative! One easy way to reduce your carbon footprint is to allow employees to work remotely. The first benefit of remote work is that it reduces emissions by taking those cars off the road by eliminating the daily commute. Another benefit to your organization is reduced office space. For instance, if you only have half of your staff in-office, then you only need a fraction of the space that you would otherwise need. If you have a completely remote workforce, you've eliminated the need for an office altogether. All of that translates into cost savings for your company, in terms of monthly rent, electric and water bills, solid waste charges, phone and Wi-Fi costs, etc. In his article titled "7 Positive Environmental Benefits of Remote Work", Eric Shad lists the following environmental benefits of remote work:

1. **No Commute Means Fewer Emissions**

    Not only does this reduce downtime and increase the amount of working time during the day, but it's also an example of one of the environmental benefits of remote work.

2. **Less Paper Usage**

    Digitizing documents for remote workers has led to less paper usage by companies across the board. Without the need for paper documents, employers can drastically reduce the appalling amount of paper used each year. But the environmental impacts of remote work and the environmental impacts of going paperless in the workplace don't end with a reduction in paper consumption. Even one saved tree can remove up to 14.7 pounds of carbon dioxide from the air, cutting greenhouse gas emissions substantially over the course of a year. This one-two punch of less waste and lower emissions makes a strong argument for continued work-from-home jobs and one that may sway employers to remain in similar work arrangements.

3. **Opportunity for Eco-Friendly Diets**

    The opportunity for an eco-friendly diet can further reduce emissions. Worldwide, cattle and meat production produces between 14.5% and 18% of total greenhouse gas emissions. Americans with work-from-home jobs have the chance to reduce their carbon footprint through eco-friendly diets. With more time to choose healthier foods and prepare meals at home, remote workers can make a huge impact on this number.

4. **Reduced Power Consumption**

Remote work makes a massive impact on power consumption around the globe. In most scenarios, this is typified through lower electricity bills for brick-and-mortar workplaces and offices. According to the World Economic Forum, power consumption has gone down overall due to work-from-home positions from the COVID-19 pandemic.

5. **Less Plastic Usage**

Raising awareness about plastic consumption since 2016, Plastic Oceans International estimates that the world produces 300 million tons of plastic a year. In addition, half of this plastic is single-use, meaning it's dumped into landfills or oceans merely a few minutes after use. Such consumption has made a negative impact on the environment, and one that will take decades or centuries to reverse. Although remote work may not directly alter that number, it again affords the opportunity to lessen the impact of plastic usage or eliminate it as much as possible. As a remote worker, you can do your part by cutting the use of plastics you normally use in an office setting.

6. **Improved Air Quality**

Remote work is vital to keeping air pollution to a minimum. During the COVID-19 pandemic, for example, a large portion of Londoners began to work from home. When this began, Breathe London data showed that emissions reduced 25% during the normal morning commute and 34% during the evening commute. Based on findings, working from home could cut 11 billion car miles per year, cutting greenhouse gas emissions by an astounding 3.3 million tons in London alone. With such an idea applied to the United States, this could equate to billions of tons of emissions reduced each year. Thus, air quality would improve not only in large city areas but in high-commuting areas such as the suburbs as well.

7. **Opportunities to Make a Positive Impact on the Environment**

Flexibility and work-life balance are amazing benefits of remote work. But with extra time, workers are also in a unique position to make an even more profound impact on the environment. Local, state, national, and international organizations provide ample volunteering positions throughout the year. Or, remote workers can take steps in their literal own backyard.

For a deeper dive into remote work statistics, check: https://globalworkplaceanalytics.com/telecommuting-statistics

In addition to remote work, an article titled "Green Your Business: 10 Ways to Reduce Your Carbon Footprint" on TerraPass.com offers the following suggestions toward reducing your emissions:

1. **Use Renewable Energy**

    A major source of greenhouse gas emissions comes from burning fossil fuels for energy. Investing in renewable energy—such as solar and wind—is an easy answer to significantly reduce the carbon footprint of your business. A variety of federal, state, and local incentives are available to help reduce the cost of renewable energy. To find information on incentives in your area, visit the Database of State Incentives for Renewables and Efficiency.

2. **Smart Lighting, Smart Working**

    Optimizing workplace lighting is another great and easy way to cut both your carbon footprint and your electricity bill. Focus on energy efficient-lighting, such as LED light bulbs and dimmable fixtures. Remember to switch off lights when they are not necessary or opt for automatic sensors to save the hassle. Take advantage of natural light as much as possible to save energy and avoid the negative health effects of excessive exposure to artificial lighting, such as heightened stress levels.

3. **Minimize Travel**

    Transportation—by ground or air—accounts for over a quarter of total greenhouse gas emissions annually. Review your company's travel practices – replace unnecessary air travel with virtual meetings and online training sessions, coordinate carpooling between employees, and choose energy-efficient models when purchasing company vehicles. A simple answer to minimizing travel emissions is to eliminate fuel use wherever possible. This includes providing the option for employees to work remotely or promoting biking to work. For the business travel you can't avoid, an investment in Carbon Offset Projects can help counteract the effects of large-scale travel.

4. Maximize Energy Efficiency

It is easy to waste electricity in the office when you're focused on getting work done. Take these precautions to maximize the efficiency of energy consumption in your office space.

- Equip your office with energy-efficient models of workplace equipment, such as monitors, computers, and printers.

- Connect desk equipment into power strips to simplify switching off all technology at the end of the day.

- Familiarize yourself with your equipment's manuals to maintain efficiency and prevent deterioration.

5. Reduce Waste

Reduce, Reuse, and Recycle. We have all heard it before. Now is a good time to put that saying into practice as decaying waste in crowded landfills releases greenhouse gasses into the atmosphere. Analyze your business procedures and pinpoint problem areas where waste production could be decreased. Choose effectively packaged products to reduce plastic waste. Minimize printing by transitioning to digital records or place convenient bins to recycle paper waste. Ink cartridges can run out as fast as you put them in, so be sure to recycle all ink cartridges, especially when you are unable to cut back on printing documents.

6. Switch to Smart Shipping

If your company relies on the shipment of products, you might want to look for greener shipping methods. Avoid shipping by air as it has lower fuel efficiency than ground delivery. Reduce the number of shipments by maximizing capacity rather than shipping in several light loads that consume more fuel.

7. Surround Yourself with Sustainable Partners

You are not alone in this fight for a greener world. If you are a small business that cannot maximize every shipment, consider partnering with other local businesses to fill shipments together. Look for partners who actively use sustainable practices. When buying company resources, limit your shopping to local vendors. This method is called near-sourcing and reduces emissions caused by transporting resources to your door. Creating sustainable business relationships will not only help to hold each company accountable, but will help reduce both of your carbon footprints in the long run.

8. Educate, Engage, and Encourage

A good business is built on teamwork. Make sure your employees are educated on the harmful effects of greenhouse gas emissions and how to reduce them. Provide motivating proof that efforts to minimize emissions have a positive impact on our environment. Connect each employee with their personal carbon footprint and engage with them in moving to a greener lifestyle. Encourage carbon footprint reduction with incentives, such as monthly competitions.

9. Save Water

Aside from avoiding high water bills, a significant amount of energy is consumed to heat water and process wastewater. Easy methods to reduce water use include installing aerated faucets, lowering water heater temperatures, and actively repairing leaks. If your business requires large amounts of hot water, consider installing a heat recovery system to recycle energy from wastewater.

10. Use Smarter Temperature Systems

Careless thermostat habits can pile onto your carbon footprint in just a few months. Be sure to adjust the office temperature by a couple of degrees with the seasons. The thermostat should be adjusted by at most 15 degrees for long periods of time when people are not present, such as overnight hours. Invest in insulation technology such as energy- efficient windows and doors. Closely watching and maintaining your heating and cooling systems is one of the best strategies to significantly decrease your carbon footprint and reduce costs. Through continuous investment in green solutions and projects to reduce carbon emissions, the goal of achieving a sustainable and economical society can become a reality.

RECs and Carbon Offsets

While there is a good chance that not all of these apply to your organization, there is also a good chance that some of them do. It is quite likely that you will not be able to bring your emissions down to zero, especially if you are including your Scope 3 emissions. But that is where 'net zero' comes into play. Once you have reduced all of your emissions to the fullest extent that you can (and this will take place over several years, rather than over the course of one year), then you will offset the remaining emissions through the employ of carbon offsets or Renewable Energy Credits (RECs). What is the difference, you ask? To answer this, I will refer you to an excellent document published by the EPA titled, "Offsets and RECs: What's the Difference?" I recommend you take time to review it when you get a chance. Below is an excerpt from that document:

- Offsets – used to address direct and indirect GHG emissions by verifying global emissions reductions at additional, external projects. Offsets (verified emissions reductions) are subtracted from organizational emissions to determine net organizational emissions.

- RECs – used to address indirect GHG emissions associated with purchased electricity (scope 2 emissions) by verifying use of zero- or low-emissions renewable sources of electricity. RECs (MWh of renewable energy) are used in the calculations of gross, market-based scope 2 emissions based on the emissions factor of the renewable generation conveyed with the REC.

What is an Offset?

An offset project is "a specific activity or set of activities intended to reduce GHG emissions, increase the storage of carbon, or enhance GHG removals from the atmosphere." The project must be deemed additional; the resulting emissions reductions must be real, permanent, and verified; and credits (i.e, offsets) issued for verified emissions reductions must be enforceable. The offset may be used to address direct and indirect emissions associated with an organization's operations (e.g., emissions from a boiler used to heat your organization's office building). The reduction in GHG emissions from one place can be used to "offset" the emissions taking place somewhere else. Offsets can be purchased by an organization to address its scope 1, 2, and 3 emissions. Offsets can be used in addition to an organization taking actions within its own operational boundary to lower emissions. Offsets are often used for meeting voluntary commitments to lower GHG emissions, where it is not feasible to lower an organization's direct or indirect emissions.

Why do Organizations Purchase Offsets?

For an organization with a voluntary commitment to reducing its emissions footprint, purchasing and retiring (that is, not re-selling) offsets can be a useful component of an overall voluntary emissions reduction strategy, alongside activities to lower the organization's direct and indirect emissions have been realized.

What is a REC?

Renewable Energy Certificates (RECs) are the legal instruments used in renewable electricity markets to account for renewable electricity and its attributes, whether that renewable electricity is installed on the organization's facility or purchased from elsewhere. The owner of a REC has exclusive rights to the attributes of one megawatt-hour (MWh) of renewable electricity and may make unique claims associated with renewable electricity that generated the REC (e.g., using or being supplied with a MWh of renewable electricity, reducing the emissions footprint associated with electricity use). Claims to the attributes of the electricity from a REC can only be made by one party. The purchase or use of renewable energy, verified with RECs, is a decision an organization makes to ensure its electricity is provided from renewable sources that produce low- or zero-emissions, thereby reducing the organization's market-based scope 2 emissions. As the physical electricity we receive through the utility grid says nothing of its origin or how it was generated, RECs play an essential role in accounting and assigning ownership to the attributes of renewable electricity generation and use. RECs legally convey the attributes of renewable electricity generation, including the emissions profile of that generation, to their owner and serve as the basis for a renewable electricity consumption claim. As such, the REC owner has exclusive rights to characterize the quantity of their purchased electricity associated with the RECs as zero-emissions electricity.

Why do Organizations Purchase RECs?

RECs can be a flexible tool to help achieve clean energy goals, lower scope 2 emissions associated with purchased electricity, and support the renewable energy market. Though RECs are the essential accounting instrument required for all renewable energy usage claims, regardless of how renewable energy is purchased or consumed, RECs can also be purchased separately from electricity and independently matched with electricity consumption. This can be an attractive option for organizations in regions where renewable energy options, such as utility green pricing / marketing programs are not offered by local suppliers, where policy support for direct engagement in renewable energy projects is lacking, or where these other options are too expensive or not suited to the organization's size or needs. By purchasing RECs and electricity separately, organizations do not need to alter existing power contracts to obtain green power. Additionally, RECs are not limited by geographic boundaries or transmission constraints. For organizations with facilities in multiple states or energy grids, a single, consolidated REC procurement can be part of an organization's strategy to efficiently meet overall clean energy goals.

RECs can be purchased from marketers or sometimes directly from renewable energy generators. Several REC marketers/environmental attribute brokers are active in REC markets, offering another approach to procurement that is increasingly being used by large purchasers. Brokers do not own the certificates, but rely on their knowledge of the market to connect buyers and sellers for a fee. Brokers also aggregate and dis-aggregate supply into customized offerings that meet specific consumer needs. This includes breaking up output from very large projects into smaller bundles as well as aggregating smaller projects offtakes into larger consolidated bundles. They can help negotiate deals that take into account an organization's unique interests. For more information on purchasing RECs, see the Guide to Purchasing Green Power. Are Offsets and RECs the Same? No. While both offsets and RECs can help an organization lower its emissions footprint, they are different instruments used for different pur-poses. Think of offsets and RECs as two tools in your sustainability toolbox – like a hammer and a saw. They are not interchangeable. Each tool is used in building a house, but each is used to accomplish spe-cific tasks. One is not more important or better than the other. Using the term "offset" (even as a verb) when discussing your REC purchases can be confusing in the mind of many listeners – confusing the action of contractually fuel-switching to low- or zero-emissions electricity with having paid for a global emissions reduction. Rather than saying your purchase of RECs is offsetting your emissions, it would be better to claim that your purchase of RECs is renewable electricity from a low- or zero-emissions resource, which reduces the emissions associated with your electricity use.

Again, ultimately, I recommend you work with a professional to measure your carbon footprint, but this information should give you a pretty good feel for what will be involved.

Sustainability is for Everyone
Sample LinkedIn article
1d ·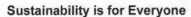

Maybe the Climate Pledge is for You

Photo by Lewis Meyers on Unsplash

The Climate Pledge, co-founded by Amazon, calls for net zero carbon by 2040. Companies and organizations that sign the Pledge agree to:

1 Regular Reporting

Measure and report greenhouse gas emissions on a regular basis;

2 Carbon Elimination

Implement decarbonization strategies in line with the Paris Agreement through real business changes and innovations, including efficiency improvements, renewable energy, materials reductions, and other carbon emission elimination strategies;

3 Credible Offsets

Neutralize any remaining emissions with additional, quantifiable, real, permanent, and socially beneficial offsets, to achieve net zero annual carbon emissions by 2040.

On June 1, 2022, ABC Company signed that pledge, along with committing to increase its overall use of clean, renewable energy to at least 25% globally by 2025.

Is it challenging? Yes. Is it necessary? Absolutely.

👍❤️👏 42   5 shares

👍 Like   💬 Comment   ↷ Share   ✈ Send

Be the first to comment on this

Chapter Takeaways

The following greenhouse gasses are counted when measuring your carbon footprint, per the Greenhouse Gas Protocol: carbon dioxide (CO_2), methane (CH_4), nitrous oxide (N_2O), hydrofluoro-carbons (HFCs), perfluorocarbons (PCFs), sulfur hexafluoride (SF_6), and nitrogen trifluoride (NF_3).

While measuring your carbon emissions is not yet *required* for public companies, it most likely will be required by the SEC very soon.

When looking for a company to work with on doing your carbon footprint measuring, do your research. Make sure they have ample experience and a good reputation. And make sure you get along with them, as you will be having a fair number of conversations and interactions with them.

Scope 1 emissions are direct emissions from owned or controlled sources (such as a furnace).

Scope 2 emissions are indirect emissions from the generation of purchased electricity, steam, heating, and cooling consumed by your company.

Scope 3 emissions include all other indirect emissions that occur, such as purchased goods and services. This includes business travel, employee commuting, use of sold products, transportation and distribution (up- and downstream), investments, etc.

Once you have completed your first greenhouse gas audit, you will have your carbon footprint baseline. Going forward, you will continue measuring this each year, with the goal of seeing a reduction year after year.

Once you have reduced all of your emissions to the fullest extent that you can (and this will take place over several years, rather than over the course of one year), then you will offset the remaining emissions through the employ of carbon offsets or Renewable Energy Credits (RECs).

Chapter 5

Employee Engagement

*T*his chapter covers what is probably my favorite aspect of any sustainability program: employee engagement. In the book *Leveraging Corporate Responsibility: The Stakeholder Route to Maximizing Business and Social Value*, authors Bhattacharya, Sen, and Korschun note that in addition to the financial benefits that sustainability practices provide, studies have found that employee retention, productivity, and overall engagement all go up. According to a study by the National Environmental Education Foundation (NEEF), almost 90 percent of employees engaged in their company's sustainability work say it enhances their job satisfaction and overall feelings about the company. While I cannot back up those statistics with my own, I can certainly say that anecdotally, this rings true for me in my own experience, based on feedback I have received from employees. Below are just a few messages from employees as examples:

"Can't wait to see all the good (our employees) do for the Earth / communities!" M.M. 4/23/21

"I wanted to tell you that I appreciate all the neat things you are doing for (our company) and the globe! I love the initiatives and look forward to participating as much as possible! Thanks for what you do!" L.W. 11/2/21

"Your department was one of the reasons I wanted to work for this company and am very excited to meet you!" J.H. 2/16/22

"...if I haven't said so lately, I absolutely LOVE all of the environmental work you do and the help you provide for everything. It's had me make so many adjustments at home as well." A.K. 3/23/22

Green Team

One thing I would strongly recommend, no matter the size of your organization, is to create a green team. A green team is basically a group of employees engaged in advancing sustainability in the organization. This applies to public and private companies, nonprofits, local governments, universities...you get the idea. This group can work towards creative solutions to environmental problems in the workplace, they can brainstorm, create incentives and games, etc. The thing I love about having a green team at work is that I can use them as a sounding board and bounce ideas off of the group.

I took an excellent certification course through the University of South Florida, Muma College of Business, called Diversity, Equity and Inclusion in the Workplace. One of the speakers was Mark Mondello, the CEO of Jabil. What he said was,

> "What we've taught ourselves over the years, is if I take six white males that come from similar socio-economic backgrounds, and put them in a room, and I asked them to solve two or three really challenging issues for our customers, and then I take six individuals that are distinctly different, really, really diverse. So again, whether it's their skin color, their gender or their physical challenges, or they have neuro diversities or their upbringing, or again, economic status. All

of that. And I put those six individuals in a room and I asked those six individuals to solve the same two or three challenges for our customers, eight times out of 10, the solutions will be deeper and more creative from the diverse group. And so that's just a simple illustration of why it's so darn important inside of a large corporation."

I would say that there are two takeaways from this insightful quote. Number one, keep in mind that if you are the only person working on your sustainability program, you are going to have exactly one perspective, and that's why a green team is so important. Number two, when you are putting that green team together, the more diverse it is, the better, the deeper, and the more comprehensive your solutions will be.

In my experience, some of "my" very best ideas weren't my ideas at all! They came from the green team. A group of employees will always have a better idea of the feeling on the floor, or the spirit of the employees, than a single employee will. I've thrown several ideas out to the group that I thought were great. Some were. Many were made far better by their input. Or the idea was massaged so thoroughly by the group that by the end of the meeting, the final idea looked nothing like the original. And many a great idea came out of the group when I simply posed a question, with no input of my own.

Use this group as a sounding board. If you have new ideas and wonder how staff would receive them, ask the group. If you need solutions to sustainability issues, ask the group. Considering incentives or contests? Ask the group. Looking to launch new initiatives, but you're not sure how? Ask the group. Want to create group events, such as street, park, or beach cleanups? Get with the group! Find out what they prefer. That way, your event will already have a solid group of participants, and you will likely get several other employees to join in.

Use this group as your environmental ambassadors. Make sure that they fully understand any upcoming initiatives, so that they can spread the word and explain them correctly. I'll give you a real-world example. At one company, we launched the "eco bin" initiative, where we replaced all of our desk trash bins with centralized waste stations.

According to Shelby Bell, Google has made several conscious efforts to improve their corporate social responsibility across the company. One of the most impactful changes Google implemented was the removal of trash cans from individual employee desks in their London office. By removing the bins, Google saw a 50% rise in recycling rates across their office. In addition to the increase in recycling, it can also save you money in custodial costs, and greatly reduce the number of plastic bags used. For example, at one company where we implemented this, we saw a 97 percent reduction in plastic bag waste and removed over 200,000 bags a year from the waste stream. Genius, right?

Upon our initial launch, not all of our employees thought this was genius! And that's being generous – there were plenty of staff who thought we were idiots. This required them to get up from their desks whenever they had to throw something away, which was frustrating to many. What I saw as a healthy side benefit (hey, now you'll remember to get up from your desk every so often, which is healthy!), they saw as a waste of their time. Especially for folks in sales, time is money, and every minute counts. It definitely took some adjustment, but luckily we had 40 or so ambassadors (green team members) who could explain the benefits and help soften the blow. Yes, we put out blogs and videos ahead of time explaining why we were doing it, and all of the benefits, but nothing beats a direct explanation from someone you work with and trust. And that's what those ambassadors were for those disgruntled employees. In case you are wondering, people quickly adjusted, and ultimately the program was a success.

Employee Engagement

Employee engagement is an integral part of our sustainability program at ABC Company. According to a study by the National Environmental Education Foundation, almost 90% of employees engaged in their company's sustainability work say that it enhances their job satisfaction and overall feelings about the company. And when employees are engaged, then the whole organization moves in the same direction, which is what we are experiencing here at ABC Company.

One of the first things we did after establishing our Sustainability program and goals was to launch an Individual Climate Pledge on Earth Day, 2020. The Individual Climate Pledge is a personal commitment that employees make to show their concern about climate change, their care for the environment, and their commitment to take personal action. Within the first three weeks, over 30% of our staff across 11 nations had taken the personal pledge. By the end of the second quarter, over 50% had taken the pledge, and over 76% of ABC Company employees have committed to the individual pledge at this writing, with more signing on weekly.

We also formed an environmental group early on, also known as a green team. The group currently has 35 passionate volunteers, and it continues to grow. The group organized four cleanups in 2021, including a scuba dive cleanup in the Tampa Bay, and a month-long cleanup initiative for remote employees across the globe. The green team also facilitated the adoption of the street our company is headquartered on, through our local government.

Photo by Jasper Garratt on Unsplash

Additionally, ABC Company held five environmentally themed contests and games in 2021, including a "No Waste" contest that spanned a month, with 50 participants from across the U.S., Singapore, the Netherlands, South Africa, Germany, Norway, Australia, the U.K. & I, and Dubai. The group is already planning 2022 contests and events, including a month-long celebration of Earth Day in April.

Finally, ABC Company acts as a sounding board and think tank for sustainability initiatives, incentives, and events. Our green team members provide feedback on zero waste initiatives, promotions, and contests. They make the sustainability program stronger and more accessible to all employees through their passion, creativity, and insight.

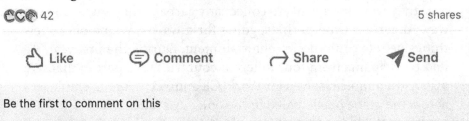

👍❤️😊 42   5 shares

👍 Like   💬 Comment   ↪ Share   ✈ Send

Be the first to comment on this

Group Activities

When you think employee engagement, think "group". This extends beyond your green team. Your green team is your core group, but you really want to engage as many employees as possible. And different activities will appeal to different employees, so try to make these efforts as varied as you can. You want to be as inclusive as possible so that people who don't enjoy group activities can do solo activities. People who don't like physical activities can do mental ones. Or people who don't live near the office can do remote activities.

Probably one of the most obvious group activities when you think about the environment is group cleanups. And I discovered at our company that our staff loved cleanups! In my first nine months there, we did five organized cleanups, and we tried to make them as diverse as possible. We had a beach cleanup. We adopted our street through our local government (and I strongly suggest this for your organization!) and cleaned up in our downtown area twice. We had a scuba cleanup in the Tampa Bay. And we cleaned up an urban farm owned by none other than Dr. Sylvia Earle, one of my very biggest heroes, and one of the kindest, most humble humans I have met. If you don't know who she is, put this book down right now, google her, and prepare to fall in love. Or prepare at least to be wowed. She's a powerhouse of goodness and achievement. But I digress.

We saw that different cleanups attracted different people, so we really were able to reach a wider audience by having a variety of cleanups. In addition to these in-person, organized cleanups, we had two remote cleanups that first year. Keep in mind that my first year at this company was 2021, so we were still knee-deep in COVID shutdowns. With that in mind, we launched a month-long event where we encouraged employees to take a bag or container with them whenever they went for a walk, to collect any garbage they saw along the way. At certain time periods, going for a walk was one of the few things people could do for entertainment. During the first year, we had participants from four different countries take part in that. We also had a remote cleanup for World Cleanup Day. Again, employees across the globe participated in the one-day event.

If you decide to pursue organized cleanups, I suggest you start by finding any local government or non-profit groups that you could connect with. Local governments (at least in the U.S.) often have adoption programs, where you can adopt a street, a mile, a park, a beach, a neighborhood, etc. Sometimes they will put up a sign with your name, which serves a dual purpose of providing positive, free advertising, in addition to providing a positive outlet for your employees and company to contribute to the community. Both governments and non-profits often provide safety equipment such as vests, gloves, and disinfectant, as well as useful materials such as trash bags, scales, and (garbage) pickers/grabbers. They usually provide sign-in sheets and liability waivers as well. Whether you team up with a group or not, you can use the following checklist as a guide to putting together a cleanup:

- Pick a date that works best for most of your employees (schedule around holidays, busy seasons, deadlines, weather events such as hurricane season, etc.)

- Pick a time of day and cleanup location (the location could be your adopted area if you have one, the area around your office, a local park or beach, etc.)

- Gather cleanup materials (safety vests, gloves, hand sanitizer, trash bags, scales, pickers/grabbers, sign-in sheets, etc.)

- Consider providing water/drinks, snacks, or even a meal

In addition to organized cleanups, contests and games are a great way to get your employees involved in sustainability and the environment. Of course, you want to tailor these contests to activities that will appeal to your staff (this is where brainstorming with your green team comes in). And again, this is a good way to reach a wider audience. For instance, our green team suggested a "show us your favorite desk plant" event, where anyone who wanted to participate could post pictures of their plants, and then a group voted for the top plants, with prizes awarded to the winners. This attracted a whole different group of staff, many of whom had not participated in any of our events up until that point. Two of our winners were from two different international offices. It was a fun, very simple way to get people from across the globe excited and engaged.

Another event inspired by one of our green team brainstorming sessions was a month called Meatless Mondays, to raise awareness about the impact meat has on the environment. According Mondaycampaigns.org, reducing consumption of meat can help contain the production of greenhouse gasses that impact climate change. It can also help lessen the demand for precious environmental resources such as land, water, and energy. The website cites the following facts about meat production:

- Livestock production creates more greenhouse gasses than the entire transportation sector – all the cars, trucks, planes, and trains in the world

- Livestock production uses 75 percent of the earth's agricultural land

- Producing ONE quarter-pound beef burger uses 425 gallons of water – enough water to fill 10 bathtubs

- Producing ONE quarter-pound beef burger uses up enough energy to power an iPhone for 6 months

- Skipping one serving of beef every Monday for a year saves the equivalent emissions to driving 348 miles in a car

Our Meatless Mondays Month drew a completely new crowd of employees, in addition to our steadfast participants. Again, many of these folks had not participated in any of our previous cleanups or the home office plant contest.

We also had a No Waste November event. We created a form with five 'no waste' challenges for them to do each day, with an additional weekly challenge, new each week. Employees filled out the form each day they participated. Each challenge had a certain number of points, and at the end of the month, the participants used their points to enter raffles for prizes. Again, we reached a wider audience, and with each new game or contest, we had more participants.

In addition to contests, consider creating celebrations or other events. For example, we turned Earth Day into a month-long celebration. We had weekly themes, with associated activities and contests. We encouraged education by recommending several environmental documentaries and championed composting through videos and educational blogs. We celebrated several international environmental days that fell during the month of April, organized group cleanups in the U.S. and U.K., and encouraged individual cleanups for our other international offices and remote employees. Another event idea we put into action was a month-long "swapapalooza." We had several tables set up in a central area of our offices (offices in six different countries all took part in the month-long swap). We had areas for books, company swag, clothing, kitchen supplies, toys, office supplies, and miscellaneous items. We also took advantage of this event to participate in GotSneakers, a program that recycles sneakers on your behalf.

I have listed just a few of the several contests and events we held. Some of them may appeal to your group, all of them may appeal, or maybe none of them do. You and your green team know your group best, so follow your hearts and get creative. The point is that your employees feel engaged and a part of your sustainability initiatives. The other point is, of course, that they (and you) have fun! It's always easier to learn when you are enjoying yourself, and so much about these contests is spreading education. Figure out what it is you want your employees to learn, and then make a contest around it, or create incentives.

Earth (Day) Month!

Photo by Fateme Alaie on Unsplash

Earth Day is April 22nd, and we at ABC Company are so excited, we will be celebrating all month! According to Earthday.org, Earth Day is widely recognized as the largest secular observance in the world, marked by more than a billion people every year as a day of action to change human behavior and create global, national, and local policy changes in order to protect our environment.

So just what is ABC Company doing to celebrate? So many things! All month, employees can take part in a company month-long cleanup initiative. This is a simple program where employees pick up trash whenever they take a walk, and then track it for prizes and bragging rights. Throughout the month, we will be sharing names of environmental non-profits for employees to donate to if they like and playing educational videos at staff meetings.

We are also having weekly themes and contests. We will kick off Earth Month with educational movie week, with prizes for the most watched videos!

National Geographic. (2016 - 2017). Sea of Hope: America's Underwater Treasures [Videos]. YouTube.

https://www.youtube.com/playlist?list=PLivjPDlt6ApQZZlf4twPLNN23U643c8On

The following week boasts both International Plant Appreciation Day on April 13th and Bat Appreciation Day on April 17th. We will share educational blogs this week, and employees will post their favorite plant and bat pictures for prizes (including a bat house).

Earth Day is April 22nd, so that week, we will host organized cleanups at several of our offices across the globe, as well as a remote costume contest to "rep the earth".

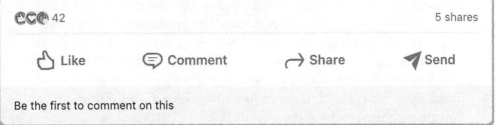

For our fourth week of themes and festivities, we will encourage employees to plant a tree on Arbor Day, April 29th, and share pictures.

And our final week will actually take place in May because when ABC Company does something, we go all out! The first week of May is International Compost Awareness Week, and we will have educational blogs this week.

How will you celebrate Earth (Day) Month?

42   5 shares

👍 Like   💬 Comment   ↪ Share   ✈ Send

Be the first to comment on this

Incentives

I mentioned incentives earlier, so what about them? Incentives are another great way to get your employees involved in your sustainability efforts. Use incentives as a tool. This tool can help you forward a message. It can help you raise awareness or reduce costs or waste. This tool can also help the environment, which ultimately is a huge part of any sustainability efforts, right? So again, decide what your goals are with regard to your employee engagement efforts, and use your incentives to get there.

One example comes directly from the TRUE Zero Waste rating system. They suggest you establish a system to collect written or verbal suggestions from all employees on your zero waste program. Included in that would be a program to identify and reward those who make outstanding contributions to reducing waste. You could offer a vacation day to the best suggestion, or a bonus to the suggestion that saves the most money. You could feature key ideas in your employee newsletter, applauding the employee or employees who contributed. Or you could take the winner, or all contributors, to lunch. The idea is to recognize them in some way; incentivize them to contribute their innovative, bold, or creative ideas. It makes the company stronger, and employee involvement greater and more committed.

Another type of sustainability incentive would be one that benefits the environment, rather than the company directly. For example, during the second year of the sustainability program I created at one corporation, we launched our renewable energy incentives, where we paid a one-time amount to any employee who purchased either a fully electric car or solar panels for their home. Our company and our employees prided ourselves on taking extreme ownership of anything we touched. We certainly "touch" the environment in so many ways. By offering these incentives, which necessarily lowered the carbon footprint of anyone who took advantage of them, our organization was thereby taking extreme ownership of the environment. Employees benefited, the environment benefited, and our organization put its money where its mouth is.

Incentives don't necessarily need to be monetary, they just need to be meaningful. For instance, a free day's vacation is not directly coming out of your organization's bottom line. Highlighting employees in your organization's newsletter is not tied to a budget line item. Acknowledging employees at a staff meeting or function, or in their personnel file, costs nothing. But all of these actions have meaning. Consult your green team and your budget and see what will work best for your company.

ABC Company Launches Clean Energy Incentives for Employees

(Photo by Nuno Marques on Unsplash)

ABC Company prides itself on taking environmental responsibility seriously. To that end, we are always looking for ways to do more.

On the personal Individual Climate Pledge, which 75% of our staff have taken at this writing, the fourth most popular option chosen across the globe was *"Reduce my personal consumption of fossil fuels: one day a week I will ride a bike, walk, carpool, or take the bus instead of driving."* This option was also in the top five of every country but one.

ABC Company heard our employees and took it to heart! As a part of ABC's continued commitment to the environment, we have recently launched a new Clean Energy Incentive. ABC Company offers two different incentives to eligible employees:

$1,000 solar incentive for the purchase or lease of solar panels for the home

$1,000 incentive for the purchase or lease of a fully electric car

ABC continues to try and make a positive impact on this beautiful blue and green marble we live on.

 42

5 shares

👍 Like   💬 Comment   ↪ Share   ✈ Send

Include Employees Across the Globe

If you have more than one office, either in other cities, or across the globe, or if you have remote employees, be sure to include them in your employee engagement initiatives. It is easy to get myopic and tailor your program for your main office or headquarters, but in order to achieve true employee engagement, you need to be sure and create a sustainability culture that makes participation possible for *all* employees. Along those same lines, keep diversity in mind. Make sure *all* of your employees are represented.

For example, if you are organizing a street cleanup at your headquarters, then encourage remote employees to do a cleanup in their neighborhood, and post pictures. If you have other offices, ask each office to organize a cleanup for their local employees. Share pictures, videos, etc. Another example would be contests—try to make these as inclusive as possible. Allow them to participate from home (or at their home office) and make sure the promotion for it is seen across all of your offices. A third example is the renewable energy incentives mentioned above. If you are launching such a program, make sure that, to the extent possible, it is applicable in all of the countries where you have offices. If that is not possible, then look for a comparable program you can offer your international employees.

The more that *all* of your employees feel recognized and included, the more they will participate, and the higher the morale will be. Make sure that those employees are represented in pictures, posts, videos, highlights, etc. We naturally want to see people who look like us represented, whether that's someone from our neighborhood, country, religion, age group, racial/national background, or our gender identity or sexual orientation. If you want a strong, robust sustainability culture, you want to make sure everyone is represented. And if you see the same usual suspects participating, then figure out how to branch out and include others. Perhaps you can survey your ERGs (employee resource groups) if you have them or survey your entire population. Find out what types of incentives appeal to them, or what activities or contests they would find interesting. Keep in mind, organizations with strong diversity climates are more likely to have employees with increased job satisfaction, higher levels of trust, and who are more engaged.

Personal Climate Pledge

One highly successful element we employed early on in our sustainability program was a personal climate pledge. A climate pledge is a commitment that you make to show your concern about climate change, your care for the environment, and your commitment to take personal action. We launched the pledge on Earth Day, and did not make it mandatory, but invited all employees to take a look at the pledge and to take it if they felt so inclined. I had a personal target of 75 percent of our employees having taken the pledge. We got to 70 percent by the third quarter of its employ, and hit 96 percent exactly one year later, on the following Earth Day. Clearly, 96 percent of our employees taking the pledge is a sign of an engaged staff. To say I was pleased would be an understatement. This was an easy way to get employees engaged and interested in the direction that our organization was going in terms of sustainability. It was also a fun way for people to feel that they were part of a solution, that they were actually doing something to improve the environment, and that they were contributing to our company's initiatives.

So, what should you put in your pledge? That depends on what is important to you and your organization regarding the planet. You could focus on one aspect of the environment, or you could pick one choice from several different aspects of climate impact. In our pledge, we offered eight choices for people to select from. They only had to choose one to have taken the pledge, but obviously, they could commit to all eight choices as well. These ranged from reducing different types of waste and consumption, increasing the use of reusables, following efficient energy use guidelines, composting, tree planting, and joining in local cleanups. We made our options pretty diverse. We tried to be as inclusive as possible. In this case, that meant including some pretty easy items to accomplish (to include those folks who were new to considering the environment) as well as some pretty challenging choices (to include those environmental veterans among us). The more challenging choices also made the pledge more meaningful. We also tried to diversify in terms of what the challenges asked of our employees. Some choices asked them to give something up; some choices asked them to change a routine; yet other choices asked them to take action in some way.

It was interesting to see the popularity of the choices depending on the country of the employee. For instance, overall, the most popular choice was reducing the amount of waste they were creating and throwing away. That was also the top choice for Dubai, India, Singapore, and the U.S. The top choice for Australia, Brazil, Germany, Japan, the Netherlands, Norway, South Africa, and the U.K. & I. was to use reusable bags. The next most popular choices were much more varied among the 12 countries. I saw this as confirmation that a variety of choices was really important so that we included all of our offices and employees in the pledge.

There are a few ways that you can get this pledge out to your employees. First, I would definitely make it electronic rather than paper – that was probably obvious. You can send a link to the pledge to all of your employees through email or your intranet. You can introduce it through your onboarding or sustainability training. You can promote it through all-staff meetings, or a fun video. Your goal is to make sure that all of your employees are at least aware of the pledge, and that it is convenient to take.

I hope you'll indulge me in sharing a few quotes from employees, which drive home once again how important sustainability is to so many people these days, and how important it is to include your employees in this endeavor. The last question on the pledge asked for any other comments, suggestions, etc. Following are a few of the more than 600 comments we received:

"This is such a great endeavor by (our company) to get everyone environmentally conscious and actively doing something to protect our planet!" D.G. 6/28/21

"Thank you so much for doing this! It's awesome! I'm so proud of (our company)!" K.R.L. 8/24/21

"I love that (our company) is dedicated to this cause and protecting mother earth. Thank you Lael!" K.G. 9/9/21

"This is one of my favorite things I love about (our company)!" E.H. 3/10/22

"I'm glad to see (our company) taking a proactive role with sustainability!" K.J. 3/21/22

Sample Personal Climate pledge

Following is an example of an individual pledge,
called The Global Climate Pledge:

The Global Climate Pledge

I have the power to make a positive difference in our climate crisis.
I will use my power to do everything I can, through my actions and
my voice, to bring about change.
I will lead and encourage others to work as a team to solve this
challenge.
Together, we will succeed!
The change begins here, with me, now.

IMPORTANT:

1) Please select at least one NEW action that you are not already doing

2) You can choose anywhere between one and all action items - only select the ones that you are committed to achieving

COMMUNITY

(These are listed first because they can make the biggest impact!)

☐ Share this Pledge and get at least one NEW person to sign

- ☐ Join/Support a local climate organization

- ☐ Vote regularly

- ☐ Vote for informed candidates that support climate action

- ☐ Vote for positive climate initiatives

- ☐ Support local businesses

- ☐ Share climate information with others

HOME

(These will also save you money!)

- ☐ Turn off all lights when not in use

- ☐ Reduce or eliminate heating/air conditioning usage

- ☐ Recycle

- ☐ Compost

- ☐ Plant your own garden

- ☐ Post "No Advertisements" sign to front door or unsubscribe*

- ☐ Replace bottled water with reusable water bottle

- ☐ Wash clothes in cold water

- ☐ Unplug electronics/appliances when not using

- ☐ Repair vs buying new products

- ☐ Use your own shopping bags *

TRANSPORTATION

(Most of these are good for your health and save money!)

☐ Walk or ride a bicycle to work *

☐ Rideshare when you travel *

☐ Telecommute *

☐ Replace some car driving with walking *

☐ Replace some car driving with electric bike *

☐ Use more public transportation

☐ Fly less *

NUTRITION

(These are good for your health, too!)

☐ Eat less *

☐ Participate in Meatless Mondays

☐ Switch from red meat to fish or chicken*

☐ Go vegetarian*

☐ Go vegan*

☐ Use leftovers for dinner once a week*

ABC Company Employees Take a Personal Climate Pledge

Photo by Ronan Furuta on Unsplash

At ABC Company, we take sustainability seriously and aim to take responsibility for how we impact the environment by being a part of the climate change solution. This concern for the environment applies not only to ABC Company as an organization but also to our employees.

As mentioned in a previous article, ABC Company signed onto The Climate Pledge On May 10, 2021.

But before that, ABC Company employees began committing to our Individual Climate Pledge launched on Earth Day, April 22, 2021.

A Climate pledge is a commitment that you make to show your concern about climate change, your care for the environment, and your commitment to take personal action.

The Individual Climate Pledge has eight categories employees can commit to including, but not limited to, reducing different types of waste and consumption, increasing the use of reusables, following efficient energy use guidelines, composting, tree planting, and joining in local cleanups.

Within the first three weeks, over 30% of our staff across 11 nations had taken the personal pledge. By the end of the second quarter, over 50% had taken the pledge, and over 70% of ABC Company employees have committed to the individual pledge at this writing, with more signing on weekly. It is our engaged employees, coupled with the commitment of our senior leadership, that has enabled ABC's sustainability program to expand so quickly and successfully. There is indeed strength in numbers.

42   5 shares

👍 Like   💬 Comment   ↪ Share   ✈ Send

Be the first to comment on this

Chapter Takeaways

In addition to the financial benefits that sustainability practices provide, studies have found that employee retention, productivity, and overall engagement all go up.

One thing I would strongly recommend, no matter the size of your organization, is to create a green team. A green team is basically a group of employees engaged in advancing sustainability in their organization. Use this group as a sounding board, and as your environmental ambassadors.

Your green team is your core group, but you really want to engage as many employees as possible. Different activities will appeal to different employees, so try to make these efforts as varied as you can. You want to be as inclusive as possible so that people who don't enjoy group activities can do solo activities.

Incentives are another great way to get your employees involved in your sustainability efforts. Use incentives as a tool. This tool can help you forward a message, raise awareness, or reduce costs or waste. This tool can also help the environment.

If you have more than one office, either in other cities, or across the globe, or if you have remote employees, be sure to include them in your employee engagement initiatives.

One highly successful element to consider adding to your sustainability program is a personal climate pledge. A Climate pledge is a commitment that you make to show your concern about climate change, your care for the environment, and your commitment to take personal action.

Chapter 6

Employee Training

Another crucial aspect of any sustainability program is employee training. This applies whether you have two employees, 20, or 20,000. The more information they have, the more effectively individuals can contribute to the cause, and also make responsible decisions in their own lives. In fact, the Green Business Bureau has this to say on the subject: "Wherever your business lies in the path to becoming a sustainable business, employee engagement and training is a must. Employee education is the way to make effective headway in sustainability because it provides the factual knowledge to make informed decisions as well as cultivate behavior change." Some essential topics you should aim to hit are: 1) your organization's sustainability targets and goals, and the program you are implementing to get there; 2) *why* these goals are important; 3) how employees can contribute to the endeavor; 4) sustainability and environmental information in general. I will discuss each of these topics below.

1) Communicate your organization's sustainability targets and goals, and the program you are implementing to get there:

Once you have established your targets and goals, these need to be communicated to your employees. This will communicate to them that they are included in your organization's important initiatives and are an important part of achieving those goals. They need to know the direction your company is headed in and will likely be thrilled to hear that you are taking steps to safeguard the environment. The more they know about your goals, the more they can help with them, and also communicate them to others inside and outside the organization. It is important to have everyone on the same page, from the bottom to the top of the organization.

2) Communicate *why* these goals are important: Share with your employees how these goals impact your company, your customers and/or investors, and the environment at large. Knowledge is power, and you want your employees as powerful and able as possible. The more they understand the importance of your program, and the many facets these goals impact, the more they will be willing and able to contribute to them. Sharing the variety of reasons these goals are important also helps to include those employees who do not necessarily feel a personal concern about the environment, for whatever reason.

3) Communicate how employees can contribute to the endeavor: You may (and likely will) have several different aspects to your sustainability program. The method of contributing to and achieving those goals and targets may differ by topic. This may mean letting employees know how to recycle correctly, how to manage energy usage most efficiently, or it may mean sharing purchasing or sustainability policies. Put as much power into their hands as possible and make it easy for them to contribute.

4) Communicate sustainability and environmental information in general: The better people understand the big picture of sustainability and the environment, the more effective they

will be as they engage in and implement your sustainability initiatives, goals, and targets. You may have employees who do not necessarily believe in climate change, but they may love animals or pollinators, or have a love for the ocean. Make room for as many employees to take interest in your program as possible.

The next several sections will cover just how to educate and train your employees. As with most things, it is not a "one size fits all" situation.

Videos

We found that a very effective tool at our company was to create very short videos, under two minutes, to kick start our employee education program. While we were working on our actual training course, which took a bit of time to write and get produced, we were able to get quite a bit of education accomplished through the use of these videos. This company happened to have a daily virtual meeting at the start of the day, which everyone attended. We were able to show these short videos here several times, which proved to be quite an effective method of disseminating information widely and quickly. If you don't have a daily meeting, then perhaps you can post videos on your intranet, or send them via email, as you would a newsletter.

"I really appreciated the videos you put out – especially the way you repeated them. That really helped. Having the confidence to recycle correctly has been really helpful." – C.H. 2/21/22

I had been with the company just a few weeks when we discovered we had a "contamination problem" in the recycling at our headquarters, so we immediately created videos on the subject. We had about seven videos that went over different areas of recycling issues, and had them played several times each, over the course of a month or two. These videos were simple, they were campy and quirky, and were shot on an iPhone. There was nothing hi-tech about them; we weren't trying to wow people, we were just trying to get crucial information across quickly. I was astounded by the amount of positive, unsolicited feedback we received on these very simple videos. The vast majority of the comments had to do with how much people learned from them. Mission accomplished!

Since that time, we've created videos for initiatives such as our centralized waste stations. We did a couple of videos ahead of time, explaining why we were making the change, which we played a few times. Then we had a video for the day that we made the switch, with a silly video giving a heartfelt goodbye to the old desk bins (which we donated to a local high school). And finally, we followed it with a "thank you/acknowledgement" video. Not everyone was happy initially with the switch to the centralized waste stations (as we anticipated), so we wanted to acknowledge those feelings, and also thank employees for making the switch work.

We also created videos for announcements. For instance, we did a series of videos for Earth Month in April, which we celebrated all the way into May. We had a video for the winter holidays, with ideas for how to celebrate more sustainably. We did a video announcing the reusable bags we made for each employee out of the building banner, and another one when we launched our bag recycling program (both plastic bags and reusable bags). We announced when we adopted beehives for our anniversary through a video. Take advantage of this simple, effective medium, and have fun with it. Take the opportunity to highlight different staff either through pictures or by asking them to do something in the video.

We also did a series of informational videos, such as how each of our international offices recycle. We in the U.S. are woefully behind some of our international counterparts. Take for example, Norway, which can recycle just about everything, including flowerpots! We shot five very short videos (under a minute each) on sustainability factoids that people may not be aware of (such as batteries being hazardous waste, and non-stop airplane flights having the lowest carbon footprint). Short videos can be very effective tools because even the most distracted individual (and in this day and age, nearly all of us are at least slightly distracted) can focus and pay attention for 30 seconds or so. Even up to two minutes if the video is silly enough or the music bopping enough.

Sample Video

Following is a sample of a very simple,
quick educational video script:

Hey team! As you know, we are striving to incorporate sustainability throughout our organization, and be more environmentally responsible. There are lots of ways to help the environment.

One of those ways is by reducing waste. To that end, please use your (company brand) reusable cups, mugs, and tumblers, or any other reusable dish, cup, or mug. Stay away from disposable cups or dishes; they can't be recycled!

You can use your reusable cups and tumblers in our break rooms every day. #Protip, bring your insulated tumbler to your favorite café and ask them to fill that up instead of using a disposable cup!

Training Course

While not required, I highly recommend you create an actual course on sustainability for your employees, tailor-made for your business. This does not need to be long, fancy, or complex; just informative. Probably one of the easiest ways to implement it is to make it a part of your orientation/onboarding process. And again, make it specific to your business. This is not the time to educate your staff on every facet of sustainability (unless you feel truly passionate about that, in which case, more power to you!).

Your training should define sustainability and any other concepts you may go over and explain why it is important to your organization. You can introduce your sustainability mission statement and/or environmental goals and commitments here. You could let them know how your organization affects the environment, and what you are doing to mitigate that, if anything. Explain what and how you recycle at your offices. If you are spread across the country, or the globe, decide whether you want one, all-encompassing training, or if you want separate ones for each region. You can also add "if you are interested" sections for those employees who feel so inclined to explore more. For instance, we had additional information on composting, pollinators, and a link to our personal pledge for people to read and take if interested.

You should decide the best delivery method for your company. If your onboarding/orientation is in person, then you may have someone give this portion of the training in the form of a talk. If your new employees do their training online, then put it into a video format or an electronic manual. This way, you can also provide links and opportunities for them to learn more about subjects they may be interested in (see my comment on composting and pollinators, above). You could also create the training in the form of a written, printed document. I would caution that this last method seems a bit counter intuitive. If you stress in your training that employees should not print unless absolutely necessary, then giving them a printed training manual may come across as hypocritical. That, and it also just isn't very environmentally friendly (or economical, for that matter). At our company, we had each new employee take the virtual training, *and* I gave a short presentation each week during the onboarding orientation meetings.

I would also encourage you to consider offering outside sustainability training for your employees. This will be seen as a great value and perk to those who are particularly environmentally conscious, or who just want to learn more. For example, through an organization called Carbonauts, we offered training that taught how to measure your personal carbon footprint, how to lower it, and why individual action is both important and effective. Our employees appreciated that this opportunity was made available to them. One of our employees shared the following: "The information that I got was super useful. It gave me a good indication of how well/bad I was doing". Another shared that the program "provoked some thought and motivation to make changes". While this training was geared toward learning about personal choices, once educated, that person will make similarly informed decisions at work, so this type of training is clearly a benefit to both the employee and the organization.

Employee Education is Crucial

CARBONAUTS

THE BIG SIX

THE 6 MOST IMPACTFUL ACTIONS FOR REDUCING YOUR FOOTPRINT

@wethecarbonauts

www.TheCarbonauts.com

From the Carbonauts website: https://www.thecarbonauts.com/

Last month, I wrote about employee engagement at ABC Company. This month, I am going to cover the importance of sustainability education for employees, and how we address it at ABC Company.

According to the Green Business Bureau, "Employee engagement and training is a must". I wholeheartedly agree. To that end, we have an internal sustainability course which all existing staff have taken, and which each new hire takes as a part of their initial training.

To date, we have 15 educational videos that we show periodically at our daily global staff meetings, with more videos in the works. Additionally, we have over 70 intranet sustainability blogs, which are essentially bite-sized posts offering green tips, tricks, and hacks.

We recently offered <u>Carbonauts</u> training to our employees, where interested staff could learn: 1) their personal carbon footprint, and 2) how to reduce that footprint. You can learn more about that training <u>here</u>. We had 28 ABC Company employees from four different countries who took the course. One student commented, *"Really great (and shocking) info. I liked how we were given different options on how we can reduce our carbon footprint that best fits our current circumstances."*

And finally, this past November, we sponsored an ABC Company TEDx event, where we showed a selection of TEDx 2021 Countdown videos over the course of one week. The TEDx Countdown was an event on sustainability and environmental issues, which counted down to the UN Climate talks (COP26) last Oct 31, 2021 – Fri, Nov 12, 2021 in Glasgow. The following quote from one attendee sums up the event nicely: *"I loved the series, the ability to watch for one hour a day, and the content was fabulous."*

Through sustainability training for all employees, we ensure that our entire company is on the same page and moving in the same direction. Through our company sustainability statement, employees know the "what" (our goals and commitments). Through education, they learn the "why" and the "how." Every single one of our employees makes a difference and is contributing to our net zero carbon emissions and zero waste goals.

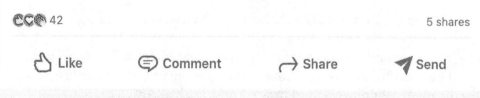

👏❤️😮 42　　　　　　　　　　　　　　　　　　　5 shares

👍 Like　　　　💬 Comment　　　　↪ Share　　　　✈ Send

Be the first to comment on this

Internal Blogs

One option that I *love* for ongoing sustainability training is the use of blogs. The easiest way to share this with your entire staff is through your intranet, but if your organization does not utilize an intranet, then you could also send emails weekly (or however often you choose to write these). If there are only a handful of you at the company, perhaps you could give a verbal "blog" at the break room table every so often, or go old school and post a weekly blog on a bulletin board. Use whatever method works for you and your organization and makes the most sense.

When I first launched this idea, I thought it would be a struggle to come up with one blog every week. On the contrary, what I have found is that it is a struggle to limit myself to only one blog a week! Sometimes these are very simple "heads-up" blogs about something happening in the local area (such as a park or beach cleanup hosted by the city). Oftentimes, they are educational blogs a few paragraphs long. Other times, they are short environmental factoids or informational pieces. I also use the blog to highlight certain national or international days – think World Cleanup Day, Arbor Day, National Bike Day, World Bee Day. The list is seemingly endless and gives you an excuse to educate your group on the topic du jour.

As of this writing, I have written well over 100 internal blogs, and I am not slowing down anytime soon. Following are several ideas for blogs, but the list is in no way exhaustive:

Informational topics

- Art made out of art repurposed items

- Feature employees doing sustainable things

- How your other offices recycle (such as international offices)

- Highlight how your employees commute sustainably

- Why litter is bad (list compelling facts)

- What your employees do for the environment

- Highlight odd things that you can recycle such as: reusable bags, office supplies, batteries, styrofoam, shoes, eyeglasses, electronics

- Your reusable swag

- Green initiatives or contests or games you're doing

- Explain your Zero Waste Plan

- Promote your sustainability or environmental commitments

- Butterfly and bee information

- Startling facts such as about single-use plastic

- Annual sustainability wrap up

- Environmentally guilt-free chocolate and wine

- Formula II electric motorsports

- Plastic waste from takeout

Educational topics

- Cooking with food scraps

- Recycling Mattresses

- Recycling plastic bags

- Recycling electronics

- Benefits of mulch (and free local resources)

- Water conservation

- How to help save the bees (and why we should)

- How to repurpose

- How to compost

Local resources and events

- Community gardens

- Advertise organized cleanups

- Electric car test drive events

- Small Business Saturday

- Hazardous waste drop off

- Free trees from the city or county

Helpful hacks and ideas

- Car hacks

- Green ways to commute

- How to plant a tree

- Green gift ideas for the holidays

- How to travel more sustainably

- Sustainable ways to clean (i.e. vinegar and baking soda)

Definitions

- Net zero carbon

- Net zero waste

- Numbers in the recycle triangle

Environmental days/weeks

- National Pollinator Week

- World Nature Conservation Day

- World Cleanup Day

- America Recycles Day

- Earth Hour

- Arbor Day

- National Bike Day

- World Bee Day

Blogs are a simple, free way to communicate consistently with your employees. Just be sure to keep up with your schedule, so that employees can rely on it, as they will come to anticipate your weekly (or routine) post. See the following chapter for some sample blogs.

Chapter Takeaways

Another crucial aspect of any sustainability program is employee training. This applies whether you have two employees, 20, or 20,000.

Creating very short videos, under two minutes, can be a very effective tool to kick-start your employee education program.

While not required, I highly recommend you create an actual course on sustainability for your employees, tailor-made for your business. This does not need to be long, fancy, or complex, just informative.

One highly effective option for ongoing sustainability training is the use of internal blogs.

Marketing and Public Relations

One aspect of your sustainability program that you do not want to overlook is marketing. The Green Business Bureau defines sustainable marketing as the process of communicating your commitment to sustainability to your customers, employees, partners, etc. Once you have your program in place, you want to be sure and make your good efforts and hard work known. This will be important to a good deal of your customers, investors, and potential employees. And you very well may inspire others to make similar moves, which is a huge bonus.

External

The value of any marketing cannot be overstated. In general, marketing your business can boost sales, maintain or improve reputation, attract new customers or investors, and establish trust in your organization, among other things. If you are a municipality, marketing can again improve reputation, establish trust, and it can be used as an educational tool. For non-profits, marketing has a lot of similar benefits, and it can help to find financial supporters, volunteers, and make your good works known. All of this holds true for marketing your sustainability efforts as well. According to Roop & Co, "...adding sustainable practices to your marketing strategy will not only attract new customers to your business but retain existing customers and build their brand loyalty and engagement over the long run."

I love how the Green Business Bureau explains why sustainable marketing works; it is because it promotes the core values that your business and your stakeholders actually value – environmental wellness, human health, resource security, fair trade, social equity, etc. They explain that it makes your company's advertising stand out in a market that is still dominated by the traditional "put-down" style of advertising. By engaging in sustainable marketing, your business will earn the trust of consumers and, in turn, their loyalty—the biggest competitive advantage of them all. Getting away from the put-down type of marketing is huge—your efforts are positive, and your marketing should match that.

I won't tell you how to market (that is a different book, written by a different author). I will just strongly encourage you, implore you, even, to include sustainability in your marketing strategy or plan. Have you made an environmental commitment? Let your external audience know. Have you reduced your paper or plastic waste by a certain percent? Scream that from the rooftops. Have you switched to sustainable resources, ingredients, or vendors? Your customers need to know this. Do you have an employee "green team" or sustainable employee incentives? Stakeholders want to know. Do your employees do regular cleanups, or follow sustainable practices in their daily life? Let your audience hear that.

And while you are sharing all of these remarkable efforts and changes, make sure the *way* you are telling your story is sustainable as well. Use electronic marketing methods if appropriate. Use social media formats such as LinkedIn and Instagram to spread the word. If applicable, use QR codes rather than paper flyers to market. If you must use paper products, be sure they are made of sustainably sourced content, *and* are recyclable. If you use swag to market, look for sustainable, diverse vendors. Make sure your swag is reusable rather than disposable. Choose products that are sustainably made and have a low impact on the environment. If there is a recycled content option, choose that. Make sure your marketing method matches the message.

If you find that your existing swag vendor(s) does not provide sustainable options, push for it. If, after requesting it, they cannot provide sustainable options, then look elsewhere, and let them know that you are doing so, and why. For example, when I went to our company's existing vendor looking for t-shirts, they had exactly one sustainable option, and it was far pricier than the established shirt. Each time I went looking for a swag item, I asked for sustainable options. A year later, they met with us to show us their new items. And in that meeting, every single item they brought was sustainable. Not only were they made of sustainable content, but they were also ethically sourced, and many of them were supplied from minority-owned businesses, and often donated a part of their proceeds to charitable organizations. And the environmentally friendly t-shirts were now cheaper than their staple t-shirts! This was a huge shift from their "business as usual," especially in the span of one year. But they heard us, and they stepped up. You can make a similar impact, and you will feel great for having done it.

Be sure to market your sustainability efforts in your recruitment program as well. Sustainability is important to potential employees, particularly from the Millennial and Gen Z demographic. According to an article by Matt Tenney in Business Leadership Today, "Sustainability is very important to employees and is an important indicator of employee engagement, retention, performance, and well-being. Employees are attracted to companies that focus on sustainability as part of their business strategy because it gives meaning to the work they do." The article points out that job seekers are looking for companies that have made tackling social and environmental issues part of their culture and business strategy. If you need further proof, consider an employee engagement study by Cone Communications, where 51 percent of employees indicated they would not work for a company that does not have strong policies addressing social or environmental sustainability issues in place. According to the same study, 74 percent of employees said their job is more fulfilling when they are given the chance to make a positive impact on social and environmental issues, with 70 percent indicating they would be more loyal to a company that helps them contribute to solutions to these issues. All of this is to say that it is crucial to include sustainability in the list of things you promote in your recruitment marketing efforts.

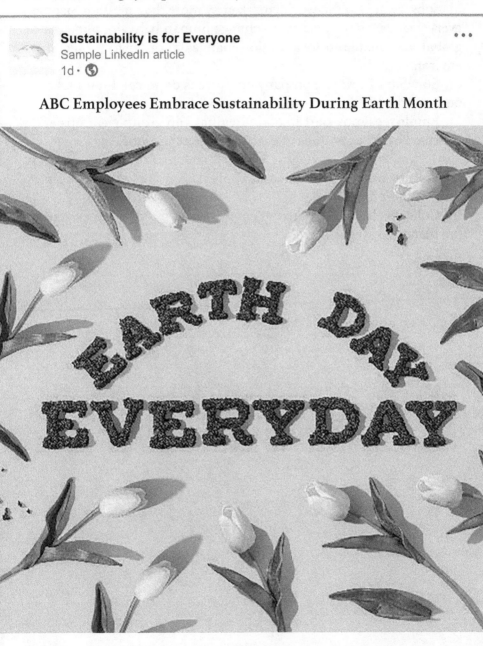

Sustainability is for Everyone
Sample LinkedIn article
1d · 🌐

ABC Employees Embrace Sustainability During Earth Month

Photo by Amy Shamblen on Unsplash

As mentioned in a previous article, ABC Company celebrated Earth Day the whole month of April, and then some! According to Earthday.org, Earth Day is widely recognized as the largest secular observance in the world, marked by more than a billion people every year as a day of action to change human behavior and create global, national, and local policy changes in order to protect our environment.

So what did ABC Company employees do to celebrate? Check out just some of the fun events that took place.

Employees took part in 60 individual and group cleanups and collected over 750 pounds of garbage across the globe.

Employees celebrated Plant Appreciation Day by sharing pictures of their favorite plants.

Collectively, ABC Company employees planted 100 trees across the planet for Arbor Day.

Employees visited our adopted beehives in the U.S., and in the Netherlands, employees each received a bee hotel!

We rounded out Earth Month during the first week of May, by celebrating International Compost Awareness Week.

All said and done, we had nearly 150 participants from 5 different countries take part in Earth Month, with prizes awarded for each of our weekly themed events throughout the month (23 winners in all).

Way to go, ABC Company employees, we are already looking forward to next year's Earth Month!

42

5 shares

 Like   Comment   Share   Send

Be the first to comment on this

Internal

Internal marketing is important as well—your employees need to know all of the good things the organization is doing. According to an article in See Change Magazine, "employees' wellbeing, sense of fulfillment, success, and co-worker connections improve when businesses adopt sustainability practices. The environmental and employee value generated through eco-friendly measures creates comfort, safety, and happiness in the office." The article further points out that employees have higher happiness and productivity rates when employers honor their health and well-being. So let your employees know that you do.

I touched on one simple way to market internally earlier, and that is through the use of blogs. This is a simple and easy way to communicate with employees on an ongoing basis. While you can use the blog to market your initiatives internally, the existence of the blog itself is another sign of your sustainability efforts. It communicates that this is a holistic sustainability program, where everyone is included. You can post these blogs on your intranet regularly or email them to your staff. Check out a couple of examples of blogs at the end of this section.

Other sources of internal marketing can be in the form of newsletters, informational videos, posters, etc. Signs around the office are an easy way for people to learn about your sustainability efforts, especially if they are strategically located. For instance, the signage on your waste bins can be a form of marketing. A sign at your copy machine encouraging people to "think before they print" is a reminder that you are keeping the environment top of mind. Creating quarterly or annual updates or wrap-ups are good marketing tools for your employees to see how far you've come as an organization. You can do this via video, newsletter, or blog.

The important thing is to communicate your sustainability program to your internal staff. It will boost morale and productivity. It will make them feel included, and it will let them know how important their contributions are. It will encourage them to follow suit and join in your sustainable efforts. And it will create ambassadors of each of them. Word of mouth is a powerful thing; do not underestimate it and do put it to work.

Sample blogs

Remember to tailor these blogs for your audience. Try to match your company voice and capture the spirit of the way your company communicates to its staff. Below are a couple of sample blogs:

Plastic Waste from Takeout Is a Big Problem—Here's What You Can Do About It

A recent study reveals a significant amount of global plastic litter is linked to takeout food products.

The study analyzed 12 million pieces of litter collected from oceans, rivers, shorelines, the sea floor, and open waters. Researchers found that 80% of items were plastic, and nearly half (44%) were related to takeout food and drinks—specifically, single-use bags, plastic bottles, food containers, and food wrappers. Yikes!! Other items included plastic caps and lids and disposable cutlery.

If you typically bring leftovers home (as I do), one of the easiest solutions is to just bring your own container whenever you go out to eat.

Keeping this new study in mind, here are some other practical suggestions from Treehugger for reducing takeout-related single-use plastics in one's day-to-day life.

1. Cook at home.

2. Call ahead...to ask: First, will they let you bring in your own containers? Second, what are the takeout containers made of?

3. Carry a zero waste food kit.

4. Say no to bottled beverages.

5. Choose packaging carefully.

6. No more grocery bags.

Let's Talk Composting!

So just what IS compost? In a nutshell, compost is decomposed organic matter. Composting is a natural process of recycling organic material such as leaves and vegetable scraps into a rich soil amendment that gardeners fondly nickname Black Gold.

If you're not already a true believer, I know composting can be intimidating. But it doesn't have to be. And it doesn't have to be fancy. And if you do it right, it won't be stinky. I collect my kitchen scraps in the soup-to-go containers I get from Chinese restaurants. I then put the scraps into one of my two outdoor composting bins (one is an actual composter that rotates, and one is a repurposed trash can with a few small holes drilled in the bottom).

Composting is a no-brainer if you have a garden (diverting waste from the landfill AND free fertilizer, hello!), but what if you don't have a garden? You can still compost! You can give it to a friend, put it in your yard, put it in a neighbor's yard (don't tell them I said that), etc.

Following are just some of the benefits of composting:

♻ Organic waste in landfills generates methane, a potent greenhouse gas. By composting wasted food and other organics, methane emissions are significantly reduced.

♻ It diverts "garbage" from the waste stream, lowering what goes to the landfill. According to the EPA, 24.1% of landfills are food waste. Yikes! We can do better, folks! And by "better," I mean send less food waste to the landfill.

♻ Compost reduces or eliminates the need for chemical fertilizers. This not only saves you money but also eliminates those chemicals from your life (and the environment), and cuts down on all that processing, bagging, shipping, etc.

♻ Compost promotes higher yields of garden crops.

♻ Compost enhances water retention in soils.

California clearly recognizes the importance of composting - they just passed a law requiring it! You can read more here (NAPL): https://www.greenmatters.com/p/california-compost-law

There are plenty of videos on Youtube to show you how to begin composting, like this one (NAPL): https://www.youtube.com/watch?v=bGRunDez1j4

> Composting Across the Globe: *(here you would pro-vide links or information for each location where you have offices).*

Other strategies

In addition to traditional marketing campaigns, there are other activities to engage in that can function to market your sustainability program and may even produce a marketable product as an end result. One such endeavor is sustainability awards. Look for local business award programs. If you are a non-profit, then you would look for appropriate awards programs for your field, or municipalities would look for county, regional, state, or federal awards aimed at local government. Awards may recognize recycling efforts, employee engagement, sustainable products, or sustainable operations. As sustainability becomes more mainstream, these categories and opportunities will only increase. If you are a nominee, a finalist, or a winner, this is newsworthy and should be marketed through press releases and social media posts.

Another worthy activity is networking groups. Join your local chamber and look for local or nationwide sustainability groups. There are several very good regional and nationwide networks for governmental sustainability staff. For businesses, there are often local sustainable business networks, and nationwide sustainability, environmental, and zero waste groups. These groups are also a great resource for best practices and moral support and can serve as a valuable sounding board. If your groups are local, this can serve as local marketing – remember what I said about word of mouth. National groups can have the same effect. Getting your organization's name out there, whether nationally or locally, can only be a benefit to your marketing strategy.

Finally, sustainability and environmental conferences are valuable activities worth considering. Primarily, these are beneficial from an informational and educational standpoint. Learning from sustainability leaders and your peers will keep you and your program up-to-date and relevant. There is a lot to be learned from a different perspective. Take advantage of this. But remember to market your organization as well, in introductions, conversations, and any presentations you give. And then, through your social media platforms, announce your plans to attend, talk about what you learned, and post pictures of the event. All of this serves to communicate to your wider audience that you are serious about your program.

Sustainability is for Everyone
Sample LinkedIn article
1d · 🌐

ABC Company is Awarded the Green Business Partnership

Photo by Jason Dent on Unsplash

In November 2021, ABC Company was awarded the *Green Business Partnership* by the University of Florida IFAS Extension, in partnership with Pinellas County. The Green Business Partnership is a voluntary assessment that recognizes businesses for their environmental stewardship and sustainable practices. It is a collaborative effort of businesses, business organizations, and county government that encourages conservation of resources, waste reduction, energy conservation, and cost savings.

Green Business Partnership
Member

Pinellas County   **UF** | IFAS Extension
UNIVERSITY *of* FLORIDA

www.pinellascountyextension.org

The application for the *Green Business Partnership* is quite rigorous and has over a dozen categories, which often require at least three indicators or measures to qualify. The assessment asks things such as the company's methods to communicate its environmental commitment to employees, its waste reduction methods, and its water conservation methods.

It also queries whether the organization has completed a waste assessment and established a recycling program which encourages recycling, and then asks for a deep dive into what additional waste reduction methods the company employs, such as composting, reducing, reusing, repurposing, etc.

Additionally, it explores the company's measures to reduce environmental impacts, its energy conservation measures (including lighting, heating, and cooling measures), and about appliance efficiencies.

We at ABC Company are not only humbled to have met the high standards dictated by the *Green Business Partnership*, but we are also proud to be a part of a community that embraces sustainability so fully and has such a professional certification available to local businesses.

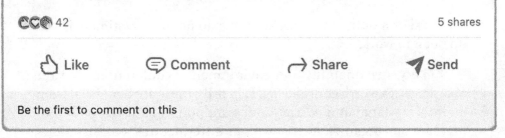

👍😍❤ 42   5 shares

👍 Like   💬 Comment   ↪ Share   ✈ Send

Be the first to comment on this

Chapter Takeaways

One aspect of your sustainability program that you do not want to overlook is marketing. The Green Business Bureau defines sustainable marketing as the process of communicating your commitment to sustainability to your customers, employees, partners, etc.

Be sure to market your sustainability efforts in your recruitment program as well. Sustainability is important to potential employees, particularly from the Millennial and Gen Z demographic.

The value of any marketing cannot be overstated. In general, marketing your business can boost sales, maintain or improve reputation, attract new customers or investors, and establish trust in your organization, among other things.

By engaging in sustainable marketing, your business will earn the trust of consumers and, in turn, their loyalty—the biggest competitive advantage of them all.

Internal marketing is important as well—your employees need to know all of the good things the organization is doing. Employees' well-being, sense of fulfillment, success and co-worker connections improve when businesses adopt sustainability practices.

In addition to traditional marketing campaigns, there are other activities to engage in that can function to market your sustainability program and may even produce a marketable product as an end result. One such endeavor is sustainability awards.

Word of mouth is a powerful thing; do not underestimate it and do put it to work.

Finally, sustainability and environmental conferences are valuable activities worth considering. Primarily, these are beneficial from an informational and educational standpoint ... but remember to market your organization as well, in introductions, conversations, and any presentations you give.

Chapter 8

Green Facilities

nother, more complex issue to consider when forwarding your sustainability goals is your facilities. This subject is made complex by the fact that so often, businesses do not own their facilities, and are often just one of many tenants in a building. This can often limit your options and ability to make sustainable choices and changes. In this chapter, we will look at several options.

According to the International Energy Agency (IEA), the buildings and construction sector accounted for 36 percent of final energy use and 39 percent of energy and process-related carbon dioxide (CO_2) emissions in 2018, 11 percent of which resulted from manufacturing building materials and products such as steel, cement, and glass. So the building you choose to rent, own, or build makes a difference. Making sure it is as green as possible can have quite a positive impact on the environment.

Before I move on to each of the options, I want to mention facilities management. Some of this has been touched on before, such as recycling, and some of it will be touched on in the next several sections, such as daylighting. One thing that applies no matter which owned/leased facility you have is the operations of the facility. This includes policies geared at equipment, such as putting your computers and printers on sleep mode after a certain amount of time and refraining from printing if possible - and choosing double-sided if you must print. These are procedures you would want to include in your sustainability policy, as discussed in Chapter 2, Create Your Mission Statement, Goals, and Procedures.

Facilities management also includes air quality issues. Some of that (such as ventilation systems) will be discussed below. But that includes cleaning supplies as well. Be sure to choose the most sustainable, environmentally friendly cleaning supplies you can. That goes for the ingredients *in* the container, as well as the container itself. Are the ingredients non-toxic? Sustainably sourced? Non-corrosive? Are the containers made from recycled content? recyclable? Returnable? As I mentioned before, take a look around you and really *look*. Watch out for blind spots. Facilities maintenance and management can easily fall within these blind spots but shouldn't.

Vacant land

If you've got the land and the funds, this can be a pretty exciting option, and indeed the ideal. Building your facilities from the ground up is the easiest and most efficient way to get an energy-efficient, "green" building which will fit your organization's needs best. You can also plan for solar this way. If you are working with an existing building, oftentimes there will be limitations on whether and how much solar you can put on the rooftop. When building yourself, you can plan around trees, calculate how much rooftop you need to run your facilities on clean energy, and then plan around that. You have the flexibility of moving equipment (such as air handlers) off the roof if need be, in order to accommodate your solar needs. And you can do it without incurring the expenses you would if you had an existing building and actually had to move mechanical equipment.

Figure 1. The Green Office Of The Future

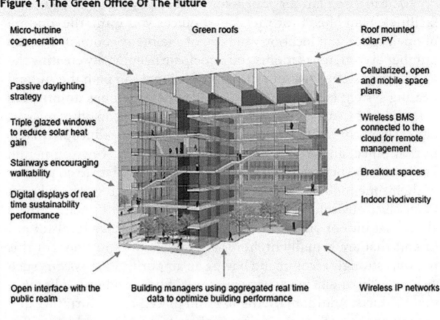

Micro-turbine co-generation

Green roofs

Roof mounted solar PV

Passive daylighting strategy

Cellularized, open and mobile space plans

Triple glazed windows to reduce solar heat gain

Wireless BMS connected to the cloud for remote management

Stairways encouraging walkability

Breakout spaces

Digital displays of real time sustainability performance

Indoor biodiversity

Open interface with the public realm

Building managers using aggregated real time data to optimize building performance

Wireless IP networks

Source: Verdantix

Green office of the future, taken from https://www.greenbiz.com/

Building your facilities yourself also allows you to plan for your exterior needs. For instance, if you will not have many employees, or few to no customers, then you do not need to build a sea of asphalt parking. And these days, there are so many environmentally friendly alternatives to asphalt, such as permeable pavers, or grass, shell, or gravel parking that is reinforced with geogrid. All of these options allow for water to percolate and reduce your heat island effect. Heat islands are urbanized areas that experience higher temperatures than surrounding, more rural areas. Structures such as buildings, roads, and other infrastructure (such as parking lots) absorb and re-emit the sun's heat, warming the area. Natural green and blue spaces such as natural landscapes, forests, and water bodies do not result in the heat island effect, so keeping as much unpaved area around your building as possible will help mitigate the heat-raising effect of the building itself.

You can also plan for your interior needs by building your own facilities. Plan ahead for the size of offices you want, the amount of open space, the location and size of the break room(s), and the number of conference rooms you anticipate needing. By creating the appropriate sizes now, your hired professional can plan the AC and heating system correctly. Moving walls later often has unintended consequences, such as reducing airflow by creating an office missing either supply or return registers (air vents). This can reduce air quality in that office, and overall. According to the EPA (Environmental Protection Agency) website, most Americans spend up to 90 percent of their time indoors and many spend most of their working hours in an office environment. Studies conducted by the EPA and others show that indoor environments sometimes can have levels of pollutants that are actually higher than levels found outside. For this reason, I strongly recommend having an air purification system, such as HEPA, "high-efficiency particulate air" filters, and/or UV lights in the AC ducts. Additionally, the use and placement of furniture and equipment can affect the delivery of air to an occupied space. For instance, the placement of heat-generating equipment, like a computer, directly under an HVAC (heating, ventilation, and air conditioning) control device such as a thermostat may cause the HVAC system to deliver too much cool air, because the thermostat senses that the area is too warm. Be sure to plan for all of this ahead of time.

Take advantage of this time to also plan lighting by making the best use of daylighting, installing fixtures for the most efficient lighting (which happen to be LEDs, at the time of this writing), etc. Daylighting is essentially the use of available indirect and direct sunlight throughout the day. Daylighting, in addition to being free, also has the benefit of improving occupant well-being. Research suggests that daylight improves not only happiness and contentedness, but also productivity. In a work environment, anything that improves productivity clearly has a value and should be at least considered.

There are plenty of other advantages to building your own offices, which your hired team of professionals can help you sift through. So when you go to hire your team, be picky. Make sure that they not only have experience building green buildings, planning for solar, etc, but that they also have the passion for it. If their hearts and minds are engaged during your project, they will get creative and resourceful, and you'll likely end up with a far better product than one that was designed by someone with little green experience or interest. You can start with either an architect or an engineer. You will eventually have both on your team, as they will work together to create your project. In addition to aesthetics and structure, your project team should recommend things such as low-flow sink fixtures and toilets to conserve water. They should talk to you about impact-resistant, Low-E (low-emissivity) insulating glass. Low-E glass has a super thin, transparent coating that blocks out nearly 100 percent of harmful UV rays. This helps protect interior features such as furniture, carpet, and window treatments from fading, it helps lower heating and cooling costs, and allows natural light inside. They are considered cost-effective, non-toxic, and long-lasting. Your team should design and dictate how your HVAC system is set to run most efficiently. They should talk to you about air quality and may suggest HEPA filters, or UV lights, in the AC system.

While architects and engineers work together, they have distinct roles. Architects generally will focus on the aesthetics, look, feel, and functionality of a structure. They do have technical knowledge about construction methods and structural design, but typically, that falls under the role of the civil engineer. Your "green" architect will likely help with identifying and recommending sustainable (interior and exterior) building materials as well. Your civil engineer will concentrate on the structural integrity of the project. They need to make sure the structure will support the loads and forces it will endure during its lifespan, and take into account natural environmental forces in your region, for instance, hurricanes, earthquakes, flooding, etc. Your "green" engineer will design in a way that reduces pollution, promotes sustainability, and protects the environment and the health of the occupants.

Finally, you can get quite creative when building from the ground up, depending on your budget. In addition to, or instead of, rooftop solar, you can consider a vegetative roof. A vegetative, or green, roof is just what it sounds like—it consists of a layer of vegetation planted over a waterproofing system, installed on top of a flat or slightly sloped roof. These are more successful in certain regions than in others. The benefits of a green roof are many: they provide shade, remove heat from the air, and reduce the temperatures of the roof surface and surrounding air. In terms of the heat island effect mentioned earlier, a green roof can moderate the heat island effect, particularly during the day.

Another fun option is a living wall. Similar to the green roof, a living wall is vegetation which grows on a vertical structure, rather than the flat or sloped roof. Unlike the roof, green walls can be interior or exterior. The benefits of interior walls are improved air quality and improved mental health. According to Heiskanen, exposure to nature has been known to decrease negative behaviors (i.e. aggression, anxiety, depression) and increase positive ones (i.e. health, cognitive capacity) through stress relief and attention restoration. The benefits to exterior green walls include improved air quality, reduction/mitigation of heat island effect, thermal benefits to buildings, attenuation of rainwater, and noise reduction. An added benefit to both the vegetative roof and living wall is the statement that it makes to the community. Without saying a thing, you have communicated your commitment to the environment, and an implied commitment to sustainable practices within the walls of your building and organization.

Green wall in the city of Westminster, London. Photo - Lael Giebel.

Owned Facilities

In terms of green facilities, the next best option after designing and building your offices is to purchase your facilities. While the layout and design of the building have already been established, owning the building still gives you a greater level of control than leasing your facilities. The best-case scenario is that you are able to purchase a green building, ideally with rooftop solar already installed.

If the building you purchase is not a green one, do not despair. You can certainly make renovations to install many of the features I listed in the previous section. This category often pertains to municipalities as well. Where local governments typically own their buildings for decades, green building renovations are one of the most effective ways that municipalities can address creating green facilities. If budget constraints are an issue, and they often are, then budget for these over time. Even one improvement a year is progress. While you can't necessarily control daylighting or how much sun is available on your roof, you can certainly install more efficient lighting, air filtration systems, low-flow sink fixtures, etc. You can consider replacing old, leaky windows with more insulated, Low-E windows. You can put your lights and HVAC system on timers to be more efficient and cost-effective. And if luck is with you, your building may be positioned in such a way that benefits rooftop solar. According to Gangolells et al, findings show that the most efficient energy renovation measures are heat pump replacement (18.1 percent) and replacement of lamps with LEDs (14.4 percent). Further, although the most effective retrofitting solutions depended on the evaluation criteria, energy, economic or environmental, 99.5 percent of the cost-effective measures also reduced emissions during the life cycle.

There are other forms of control that you have with a purchased building that work to your advantage as well. For instance, if you own your building, then you can get the most accurate numbers for your zero waste plan. You can use tonnage numbers from your solid waste providers with confidence, to measure your trash and recycling weights. You can trust that your energy numbers for your reporting and environmental commitments, such as net-zero carbon by a certain year, are accurate, as you are the only customer using energy in the building. This is a beneficial level of control that you unfortunately will not have in a leased building with multiple tenants.

Leased – Single Tenant

While you have less control with leased buildings than over built or purchased ones, you still have options. Most landlords will welcome building improvements that are paid for by tenants, so making many of the same improvements mentioned in the previous section should not be an issue. Consider installing more efficient lighting, air filtration systems, low-flow sink fixtures, etc. You may want to consider replacing old, leaky windows with more insulated, Low-E windows. You can put your lights and HVAC system on timers to be more efficient and cost-effective. One downside is, of course, that if you move, then the cost of those improvements is essentially money left on the table. For this reason, you may not want to invest in rooftop solar, but you could have a conversation with the landlord to encourage them to make the investment.

Several of the other control benefits mentioned in the previous section still apply when you are the only tenant in a leased building. For instance, if you are the only tenant in the building, then you can still get the most accurate numbers for your zero waste plan. You can still use tonnage numbers from your solid waste providers with confidence, to measure your trash and recycling weights. And you can still trust that your energy numbers for your reporting and environmental commitments (such as net-zero carbon by a certain year) are accurate, as you are the only customer using energy in the building.

Leased – Multiple Tenants

If I have painted a bleak picture of this last category, I apologize. While this form of occupancy offers the least amount of control, you can still operate in a sustainable manner; you may just need to get more creative, and put in a bit more effort to get there. Start by looking for a green building. If that fails, then read on for other potential solutions.

This was, in fact, my situation when implementing our corporate sustainability program. Our corporate headquarters were situated in two high-rise buildings shared with at least one other tenant. In order to achieve our environmental targets and commitments, this called for a bit more effort and creativity. For instance, we had to routinely weigh each of our garbage and recycle bin contents to get accurate zero waste numbers. We had to perform certain calculations and estimations to get our energy usage numbers. And once environmental required reporting was proposed by the SEC, we installed submeters to get an even more accurate measurement of our energy usage in both buildings. Sub-meters collect actual energy usage per floor, which is not possible through a standard energy bill.

Rather than installing solar, we were able to negotiate with the landlord of one of our buildings to take advantage of a program through our energy provider called Clear Energy Connection, which allows the customer to essentially purchase clean energy without installing rooftop solar. I encourage you to check for similar programs in your area. If they exist, then have a conversation with your landlord, and encourage them to apply. This could even become a requirement during your lease negotiations.

As with single-tenant occupancy, several of the other control benefits mentioned in the section above still apply in a multi-tenant building. Consider installing more efficient lighting, air filtration systems, low-flow sink fixtures, etc. You may want to consider replacing old, leaky windows with more insulated, Low-E windows. You can put your lights and HVAC system on timers to be more efficient and cost-effective. Most, if not all, of these improvements will be welcomed by the landlord if you, as the tenant, are the one paying for them.

Regardless of what form of occupancy you have, owned, leased, etc, there are green facility options for you. Do your homework, investigate, and get creative. Consider engaging a design team, whether to build a new building or renovate your owned or leased building. If you can't afford all of the renovations now, then prioritize them, and budget for future years. You will get there, and you will be pleased you made the investment and the effort.

Real Estate Business

So far in this chapter, I have addressed tenant needs and concerns. But what if you are the landlord, or perhaps a real estate developer or investor? I haven't forgotten you! Below are several compelling real estate benefits of green building. While the article is aimed at green building certification, the benefits apply whether the building is green building certified or is simply built to green building certification standards. Following are six benefits to green building according to Awair.com:

- Lower Operating Costs

  Energy efficiency is one of the key principles behind many green building certifications. In addition to implementing energy-efficient heating, cooling, and ventilation systems, many green building projects are designed to harness natural resources like light and air. By being more strategic about window placement, mindful about energy sources and appliances, and by creating natural ventilation options, developers save on utility bills down the road. In fact, a study done by the General Services Administration (GSA) found that operational costs for green buildings were 19 percent lower than the industry average.

- Tax Incentives and Funding Opportunities

  Many towns and cities offer tax benefits and funding opportunities to encourage developers to create more energy-efficient and sustainable buildings. These benefits can include temporary property tax exemptions on green renovations, tax rebates, permitting fee reductions, zoning allowances, EPA Grants, and special mortgage programs.

- Structural Benefits

  In addition to financial incentives, some municipalities offer structural incentives to projects that support statewide sustainability goals. These can include an expedited permitting process, or floor area ratio, height, and density bonuses that are awarded based on green building credentials.

• Better Occupancy Rates

Green building certifications such as LEED, WELL, Fitwel, and LBC are performance-driven certifications. In other words, buildings must be monitored after certification to ensure that green initiatives are having the intended impact. Although this continuous monitoring requires a long-term commitment, green properties tend to earn higher occupant ratings for air quality, cleanliness, maintenance, indoor lighting, natural light, acoustics, and general workplace/building satisfaction. These higher-than-average ratings help to reduce occupant turnover and inspire more organic referrals — both things which lead to higher occupancy rates.

• Higher Rental Rates

Due to their abundance of natural light and commitment to occupant health, green buildings tend to be more desirable than traditional properties. This high demand means that property owners can charge higher rental premiums, which can offset project costs. A study of over 7,000 commercial buildings in prime metropolitan areas found that LEED certified properties earned an average of 2.9 percent more rent than non-certified buildings.

• Lower Emissions

This list wouldn't be complete without mentioning the most far-reaching benefit of greener building practices: lower carbon emissions. In addition to benefiting your company's bottom line and protecting building occupants, greener building practices help to lower local emission totals, thereby benefiting community and environmental health. According to a GSA report, LEED certified buildings emitted 36 percent less CO_2 compared to national building emission averages. The building sector is responsible for 43 percent of all CO_2 emissions in the U.S. (more than transportation or industry), so committing to green building initiatives can have a profound impact. Championing such initiatives can also generate positive brand perception, reinforce brand values, and inspire closer ties with the surrounding community.

Chapter Takeaways

The buildings and construction sector accounted for 36 percent of final energy use and 39 percent of energy and process-related carbon dioxide (CO_2) emissions in 2018, 11 percent of which resulted from manufacturing building materials and products such as steel, cement, and glass.

One thing that applies no matter which owned/leased facility you have is the need for green, sustainable operations of the facility.

Building your facilities from the ground up is the easiest and most efficient way to get an energy-efficient, "green" building, which will fit your organization's needs best.

Most Americans spend up to 90 percent of their time indoors, and many spend most of their working hours in an office environment. Studies conducted by the EPA and others show that indoor environments sometimes can have levels of pollutants that are actually higher than levels found outside.

An added benefit to both the vegetative roof and living wall is the statement that it makes to the community. Without saying a thing, you have communicated your commitment to the environment, and an implied commitment to sustainable practices within the walls of your building and organization.

In terms of green facilities, the next best option after designing and building your offices is to purchase your facilities. While the layout and design of the building have already been established, owning the building still gives you a greater level of control than leasing your facilities.

While you have less control with leased buildings than with built or purchased ones, you still have options.

In a leased building, rather than installing solar, look for an energy provider or program in your area which allows the customer to essentially purchase clean energy without installing rooftop solar. If such a program exists, have a conversation with your landlord, and encourage them to apply.

Greening Your Product(s)

This chapter covers your actual product, if you have one. If you provide a service, rather than a product, then it likely will not apply to you. Having said that, I think there is a good deal of interesting, if not valuable, information located within this chapter, and it is worth reading! The topic of green products is so vast I almost hesitate mentioning it. The list of products you may produce is seemingly limitless, so I won't try to predict them here. What I will try and tackle is the way you go about producing and packaging your product(s). And actually, this applies whether your product itself is considered a "green product," such as shampoo bars, which eliminate plastic containers, or just a product that you would like to make more environmentally friendly.

What is a green product?

Just what is a green product? A green product is one which is sustainable and designed to minimize its environmental impacts during its whole life-cycle and beyond. The two key elements are maximizing resource efficiency, while also reducing waste. According to Prinona Das, some of the characteristics of a green product are:

- Grown without the use of toxic chemicals and within hygienic conditions

- Can be recycled, reused, and is biodegradable in nature

- Comes with eco-friendly packing

- Uses the least resources

- Is eco-efficient

- Has reduced or zero carbon footprint

- Has reduced or zero plastic footprint

- May be certified by organizations like Energy star, Forest Stewardship Council, etc

Why create sustainable products and packaging? I am probably preaching to the choir at this point, but I will refer to an article published by Business News Daily appropriately titled "Most Consumers Want Sustainable Products and Packaging" to answer that question. There are a couple of key takeaways from the article worth mentioning, the first being that many customers are willing to pay more for sustainable products with high-quality, environmentally friendly packaging. The second key takeaway is that consumers are more attracted to brands with sustainable practices and products – and those businesses turn a profit.

Why green products and packaging matter: 9 out of 10 people worldwide breathe polluted air, 500 Billion to 1 Trillion plastic bags end up in land- fi lls each year worldwide, and A plastic bag can take up to 1,000 years to decompose A study from 2015 says that 73% of the con- sumers across 60 countries are willing to pay more for sustainable products. –Prinona Das, https://www. feedough.com/green-product/

Circular Economy

To the best of your ability, strive to create a circular economy. A circular economy, as defined in the Save Our Seas 2.0 Act, refers to an economy that uses a systems-focused approach and involves industrial processes and economic activities that are restorative or regenerative by design, enable resources used in such processes and activities to maintain their highest value for as long as possible, and aim for the elimination of waste through the superior design of materials, products, and systems (including business models). According to the EPA, the circular economy is a change to the model in which resources are mined, made into products, and then become waste. A circular economy reduces material use, redesigns materials to be less resource intensive, and recaptures "waste" as a resource to manufacture new materials and products. The circular economy is based on the Cradle-to-Cradle principle. Cradle-to-cradle (or C2C) is a way of designing products or processes that work more like natural systems. This design method is intended to replace a make-take-dispose approach, which begins with new raw materials mined from the earth and ends with piles of garbage. Cradle-to-cradle as a concept is often credited to Swiss architect Walter Stahel. Today, the term "cradle-to-cradle" is a registered trademark of McDonough Braungart Design Chemistry (MBDC) consultants.

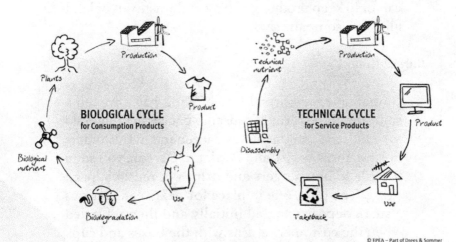

Cradle-to-Cradle cycle taken from the EPEA:
https://epea.com/en/about-us/cradle-to-cradle

To put that into layman's terms, in a circular economy, you would design your products to be reusable. One example would be a manufacturer of electrical devices. In this case, they would design the devices in such a way that they are easier to repair. The products and raw materials would be reused as much as possible. Then at the end of the effective life cycle, the manufacturer would take the devices back to repurpose or dispose of in a sustainable manner. For example, recycling plastic into pellets for making new plastic products. Following are two real-world examples highlighted on the World Economic Forum website:

Adidas

Sportswear multinational Adidas has a range of footwear designed with recycling in mind. Its UltraBoost DNA Loop shoes are made from just one material – thermoplastic polyurethane (TPU). No glue is used in its manufacture, instead, it is assembled using high temperatures. On its website, Adidas describes the UltraBoost Loop as the shoes customers will never own, but will instead return once they are finished with them. "If the end can become the beginning, we can help keep products in play and waste out of landfills," the company says.

Burger King

Global takeaway brand Burger King has unveiled a solution in the form of reusable packaging intended to reduce the amount of waste it generates. Customers in New York, Tokyo, and Portland, Oregon, will soon be able to buy burgers and drinks in reusable packaging. The plan, one in place for next year, features a small deposit charged initially and then refunded when the customer returns with the boxes and cups, which are taken away for cleaning and processing via the zero-waste e-commerce system Loop.

With sustainability in mind, take into account the materials your product includes or is made of. Are the materials recyclable? Recycled? Sustainably sourced? Non-toxic? Are they relatively unprocessed? If you produce food, are the ingredients sustainably and/or organically grown? Are they healthy? Environmentally friendly? If you produce clothing...well, that's a whole book in itself! But to start, are you sourcing ethical suppliers? Using non-toxic dyes, or not dying your materials? Does your fabric use minimal processing? Or is it recycled or repurposed? Is it natural fiber material, and is it organically grown and obtained in an environmentally friendly way? And finally, how will your product's end of life be handled? Is it recyclable? Will you take it back and upcycle it, or dispose of it responsibly? If you produce something edible, you've lucked out here!

If you have a product in mind, consider some way or ways to make it more environmentally friendly. Greendotbioplastics.com makes the following suggestions for creating a more sustainable product (which may or may not apply to your product, depending on its content):

- Source materials more locally to decrease transportation emissions and costs.

- Use reclaimed, post-industrial grades of plastic instead of virgin materials when possible.

- Reduce the amount of material needed through part design.

- When possible, select a compostable plastic.

- Select minimalistic packaging made from materials that can be, or have already been, recycled or reclaimed.

Also, look into some of the newer "green" materials on the market. They are amazing! Consider, for example, hemp, pineapple leather (Piñatex), mushroom leather (Mylo), recycled wool, etc. Mycelium (a fungus found in mushrooms) is particularly intriguing. According to the Mylo website, Mycelium can be used to make building materials fire-resistant, stronger, and lighter. It can be used in the fashion industry to mimic the look, texture, and utility of leather. In some cases, it can even be used as a bonding agent for building materials, such as brick. Mycelium is an eco-friendly, sustainable, and renewable resource. Because of its inherent properties, it can be recycled and regrown time and time again. With many industries in search of more sustainable solutions, mycelium provides a world of endless possibilities.

Another aspect of creating sustainable and ethical products is sourcing them from local suppliers, and minority-owned businesses, where possible. Local food or products don't have to travel as far, thereby reducing greenhouse gas emissions. Buying locally also benefits the local economy. Similarly, shopping at minority or women-owned companies frequently puts cash into the local economy.

Packaging

Similar questions apply for your packaging. Are the materials recyclable? Recycled? Sustainably sourced? Non-toxic? Undyed, unprocessed, or less processed? How will the packaging be disposed of? Can it be repurposed? And once you have landed on all of the best options, how can it be improved from there? Can plastic packaging be replaced by paper, or cardboard, or biodegradable materials? If you use plastic containers, can they be replaced by glass? Do you need as much packaging as you are planning to use? Continue to ask questions, and you will be headed in the right direction. And get creative. For instance, at one company that produced eco-friendly products, we shredded our excess catalogs and non-secure papers and used that material to pack the goods when we shipped them to our customers. According to the Business News Daily article referenced earlier in this chapter, in one survey, 77 percent of respondents said plastic is the least environmentally responsible type of packaging. Keep that in mind as you move forward in designing not only your product but the packaging as well.

Francesca Nicasio's blog titled, "9 Environmentally Friendly Packaging Materials to Help Your Business Go Green" offers several ideas to consider for sustainable packaging; nine ideas, to be exact:

- Compostable packaging – meaning it is able to naturally decompose back into the earth, ideally without leaving any toxic residue. Compostable packaging materials are usually made from plant-based materials (like corn, sugar cane, or bamboo) and/or bio-poly mailers. It's important to note that for a material to be truly considered compostable, it should be able to break down in home compost within 180 days and 90 days in commercial composting conditions.

- Recycled packaging—self-explanatory.

- Corrugated packaging—this refers to box fibers made mainly from trees and old corrugated containers.

- Glassine packaging—this is transparent paper packaging manufactured from wood pulp, making it recyclable and bio-degradable. It's also pH neutral and acid-free.

- Cellulose packaging—this is made from natural sources like hemp, wood, and cotton. The material is biodegradable and compostable, making it a sustainable alternative to plastic. Food brands, in particular, prefer cellulose packaging because of its moisture-resistant properties.

- Cornstarch packaging—just like it sounds, this refers to materials made out of cornstarch. It comes from renewable sources and doesn't contain harmful toxins, making it biodegradable and sustainable. Cornstarch can also be used to make bio-degradable packing peanuts, which is a great alternative to bubble wrap and styrofoam.

- Mushroom packaging—this is another cool alternative to Styrofoam. Mushroom packaging is made from mycelium—a fungus found in mushrooms. The result is a sturdy packaging material that can hold products and keep them in place.

- Kraft paper—unlike regular paper, kraft materials use all types of wood, including resinous pine, which is typically left out when creating regular paper products. Almost all of the chemicals that go into making kraft paper can be reused, so the manufacturing process is more sustainable.

- Green Cell Foam—a bio-based foam material made from corn. You can dispose of it by dissolving it in water or by composting the material at home or at industrial facilities.

Brag!

Okay, you've chosen your sustainable materials and ethical packaging, now it's time to brag! In everything you do, be sure to make your good works known. Talk about the decisions you've made, materials you selected, and how you got there. Put messages on your packaging, on your products, on your shipping invoices, on your tags... you get the idea. Share this on your website and social media as well. And don't forget about your staff! Make sure your employees know how sustainable your product(s) and packaging are so that they can spread the good word as well.

Chapter Takeaways

Many customers are willing to pay more for sustainable products with high-quality, environmentally friendly packaging, and consumers are more attracted to brands with sustainable practices and products—and those businesses turn a profit.

A circular economy refers to an economy that uses a systems-focused approach and involves industrial processes and economic activities that are restorative or regenerative by design, enables resources used in such processes and activities to maintain their highest value for as long as possible, and aim for the elimination of waste through the superior design of materials, products, and systems (including business models).

Cradle-to-cradle (or C2C) is a way of designing products or processes that work more like natural systems. This design method is intended to replace a make-take-dispose approach, which begins with new raw materials mined from the earth and ends with piles of garbage.

Take into account the materials your product includes or is made of. Are the materials recyclable? Recycled? Sustainably sourced? Non-toxic? Are they relatively unprocessed?

Look into some of the amazing, newer 'green' materials on the market. Consider hemp, pineapple leather (Piñatex), mushroom leather (Mylo), recycled wool, etc.

Are your packaging materials recyclable? Recycled? Sustainably sourced? Non-toxic? Undyed, unprocessed, or less processed? How will the packaging be disposed of? Can it be repurposed?

Brag about the decisions you have made, materials you selected, and how you got there. Put messages on your website and social media, on your packaging, on your products, on your shipping invoices, on your tags, etc.

Chapter 10

Conclusion

Congratulations, you have made it through this book, and are presumably on your way to creating and implementing a sustainability program at your company. Well done on taking the first steps toward reducing your company's negative impact on the environment. That is no small feat. No matter how many or how few suggestions you take away from this book and apply at your company, you are making progress. I started this book by suggesting you "just start"—start somewhere. By this point, you should be ready to do just that. Jump in with two feet, or at least one, and start your sustainability journey.

There are several recurring themes that wove their way through many of the chapters. First, time and again, there was the notion of making this your own. Make sure the program you create is relevant to your company. Make sure it fits your company's culture and goals. Make sure you have buy-in from the top, and engagement from staff. Make sure your internal communications fit your company's voice, and your external communications are tailored to your audience.

Another recurring theme is that of creating a judgment-free zone. I cautioned that for those people who do not believe that protecting the environment is important, you need to give them the space to believe that. Do that, and they most likely will not feel compelled to resist your efforts. If you make them "wrong" then they will fight you every step of the way to be "right" (#protip, this goes a long way with raising kids, as well!). Alienating your employees, your executives, your customers (or your kids!) will never get you anywhere. Not anywhere good, anyway.

While the book began with a somewhat discouraging look at the environment in Chapter 1, State of the Environment, you are now equipped and strategically poised to become a part of the solution. Every positive change you make, whether as a company or as an individual, makes a difference. Along those lines, and to drive this point home, I will share a post I wrote on LinkedIn for Earth Day 2022, where I shared some ideas on how individuals can live more sustainably:

> I think a common obstacle is just feeling overwhelmed. Like, "...there is so much to do, and I can't do it all, so I won't do any of it". It is understandable because helping the environment is a broad subject. Start with the things that come easy and make sense to you, then move on from there. You'll burn through that paralysis and will likely find that it is easier to live a more sustainable lifestyle than you realized.

Here are some ideas:

> I think you can get a pretty big bang for your buck by reducing the amount of meat you consume, composting rather than throwing away food, using reusable bags at the store, reducing the amount of plastic you use, from plastic bags, to single-use water bottles, to disposable utensils. But again, start with what speaks to you. For example, if you care about wildlife, then eliminate pesticides

in your yard, put up a bat box or mason bee house, or pick up garbage in your neighborhood.

Remember that being frugal is often also a good way to be sustainable. For instance:

-Beans are much cheaper than meat, they are also healthier, and are easier on the environment (the carbon footprint of beans is a fraction of beef's carbon footprint).

-Buying food from the bulk bins is typically less expensive and is also more sustainable because you avoid the individual packaging.

-Riding a bike is cheaper than driving a car. It is also healthier, and it is better for the environment.

-Turning off the water while you brush your teeth saves you money and is better for the environment.

The biggest thing to remember is that every little bit counts – don't beat yourself up about what you are not doing. Rather, feel good about what you are doing. And then see if you can do more!

I say the same to you as you embark on creating your company's sustainability program. It is easy to feel overwhelmed about where to start (although I hope this is no longer the case after reading this book). Don't beat yourself up about what you are not doing. Rather, feel good about what you are doing. And then see if you can do more!

Remember that one of the most effective tools in your tool belt is your employees! They will be a huge part of your success; do not underestimate them. Create your green team and use this group as a sounding board. If you have new ideas and wonder how staff would receive them, ask the group. If you need solutions to sustainability issues, ask the group. Considering incentives or contests? Ask the group. Looking to launch new initiatives, but you're not sure how? Ask the group. Want to create group events, such as street, park, or beach cleanups? Get with the group! Find out what they prefer. That way your event will already have a solid group of participants, and you will likely get several other employees to join in.

There is strength in numbers, and a small group of passionate employees can create some pretty powerful positive momentum. And keep in mind the statistics noted earlier in the book that show how important sustainability is with regard to employee hiring, morale, and retention:

> According to a report by PWC titled *"The future of work: A journey to 2022"*, 65 percent of people in the U.S., Germany, India, China, and the U.K. want to work for an organization with a strong social conscience. According to online magazine *Worklife,* new research (as of 2021) from global recruitment firm Robert Walters indicates 34 percent of U.K. office workers would refuse a job offer if a company's environmental, sustainability, or climate control values do not align with their own. In the U.S., the figure is even higher: 41 percent. France and Chile (both at 53 percent) top the list, closely followed by Switzerland (52 percent).

> According to a study by the National Environmental Education Foundation (NEEF), almost 90 percent of employees engaged in their company's sustainability work say it enhances their job satisfaction and overall feelings about the company.

> According to an employee engagement study by Cone Communications, 51 percent of employees indicated they would not work for a company that does not have strong policies addressing social or environmental sustainability issues in place. According to the same study, 74 percent of employees said their job is more

fulfilling when they are given the chance to make a positive impact on social and environmental issues, with 70 percent indicating they would be more loyal to a company that helps them contribute to solutions to these issues. All of this is to say that it is crucial to include sustainability in the list of things you promote in your recruitment marketing efforts.

If you've gotten this far, but you are not actually sure *what* you want to do for your business, only *that* you want it to be green, then consider the following suggestions from Max Freedman from an article titled "23 Green Business Ideas for Eco-Minded Entrepreneurs":

1. Ink Refill Business

Starting an ink-refill business can not only be a highly profitable decision, it can be an environmentally conscious one, too. You might question whether refilling ink cartridges truly helps the environment, considering the amount of paper that is wasted each year. However, by reusing old ink cartridges, there is less non-biodegradable waste accumulating in landfills. Paper is still necessary in the business world, but empty ink containers are not.

2. Environmental Publications

If you love to write, start your own environmentally minded publication. Your actions can make a big difference in the world. By debunking popular myths and sharing the truth about the world we live in, you can help consumers rethink how their actions affect the planet.

3. Green Finance

Green finance focuses on supporting local, community-level projects with an emphasis on sustainable, ecologically friendly agriculture. Green finance is also typically concerned with providing educational opportunities, funding for artistic endeavors, and projects that support local ecology. Green finance is preoccupied with social profitability. While monetary profit remains important, the goal of green finance is to support beneficial projects that provide value to the local community and ecology.

4. Eco-Friendly Retail

Consumer rewards programs are popular among retailers, and e-commerce site EcoPlum is no exception. With every purchase, customers earn EcoChipz, which are redeemable for either rewards or a donation to various environmental causes. Each product sold also carries a third-party green certification or an equivalent eco-label. Besides selling sustainably sourced products, EcoPlum produces educational content, including monthly columns by industry experts, local green business listings, recycling information, eco tips, and book and video recommendations. If you're considering opening a retail store, consider partnering with a company that has similar values as you and your customers.

5. Sustainable Construction Materials

You might not think of construction as sustainable, but some companies now provide recycled materials for use in projects like infrastructure repair. Axion, for example, with its eco-friendly products, hopes to change the way companies think about rebuilding America's infrastructure. The company's railroad ties and pilings are made from recycled plastic from consumer and industrial uses rather than non-sustainable materials like steel and concrete. Axion is currently working with major partners like Long Island Rail Road to improve infrastructure safely and sustainably in the United States.

6. Organic Catering

A great way for eco-friendly foodies to share their passion for food and the environment is to start an organic catering company. By catering local events and business luncheons with foods containing organic and locally grown ingredients, free-range meats, and vegan, gluten-free, and paleo meal options, you'll appeal to nature lovers and health and wellness enthusiasts alike.

Be sure, though, to minimize the impact on the environment by avoiding plastic and paper goods as much as possible and composting food waste.

7. Eco-friendly Beauty Salon

If cosmetology is your passion, start a beauty business that's Mother Nature-approved. Organic and vegan hair and beauty products are popping up everywhere. A way to make this trend work for you is to open an eco-friendly beauty salon. You can open a hair salon that uses all-natural shampoos and conditioners or a nail salon that uses environmentally friendly and vegan polishes and spa treatments.

8. Eco-friendly Landscaping

Professional landscaping may make your lawn and garden look nice, but all of that maintenance isn't necessarily great for the environment. With some eco-friendly advice and know-how, you can help homeowners make their yards literally and figuratively greener. SheKnows recommends synthetic turf, drought-resistant plants, and strategically placed trees for a lawn that saves water, energy, and money.

9. Sustainable Event Planning

Whether they're big or small, meetings and events can generate large amounts of waste and consume valuable resources. Green event planners use their expertise and event-planning skills to find eco-friendly venues, materials, and accommodations. Sustainable event management benefits more than just the planet. There are financial advantages, plus it generates a positive image for event organizers, vendors, and stakeholders while raising awareness and inspiring change in the community.

10. Bicycle Repair and Refurbishing

Biking short distances instead of driving is better for the environment and your health. Like most modes of transportation, bicycles occasionally need a tune-up.

You could be the expert cyclists come to when their bikes need repairing or maintenance. If you have some extra space, you could purchase inexpensive older bikes, fix them up and sell them for a profit.

11. Handmade All-natural/Organic Products

Soaps, cosmetics, and cleaning products are just a few of the household products that can be made using common organic materials. Sure, anyone can find a recipe for a sugar scrub or vinegar-based cleaning solution and do it themselves, but if you package and sell them in sets, your customers conveniently have those all-natural products at their fingertips. Local markets and events are a good place to sell, or you could start an online store.

12. Eco-consulting

Are you an expert on green living? Start an eco-consulting service. Consultants evaluate homes and offices, and offer solutions to make them more environmentally friendly. You could advise clients on switching their home appliances to more energy-efficient machines or implement a recycling program. To further boost your credibility, become a certified eco-consultant.

13. Farmer's Market Vendor

Thanks to the organic movement, those with a green thumb have a golden opportunity to earn money by selling non-GMO, pesticide-free produce at their local farmer's market.

Selling naturally grown fruits and vegetables gives you a distinct advantage over competing growers who use conventional farming methods, including pesticides. You may have to be approved and/or get certified by your local board of health first before you can begin selling.

14. Green Housekeeping Services

For working parents, cleaning the house can be at the bottom of the to-do list. Market yourself as the green solution to their housekeeping woes by offering services that range from light dusting to heavy-duty chores like cleaning the kitchen and bathroom, using only approved all-natural and eco-friendly cleaning products.

Charge an hourly rate or create your own service packages for a flat fee. Remember, your clients are giving you access to their homes. Build a trustworthy reputation with people you know first before advertising to strangers.

15. "Upcycled" Furniture

Don't throw out your old, broken furniture. With basic templates and access to power tools, you can break down and reassemble chairs, tables, and dressers into new pieces that you can paint and sell. Shelving and storage units are easy to make from wood scraps, and depending on the item, you might even be able to fully restore a unique and valuable piece of furniture.

Alternatively, you could reupholster old chairs and couches, giving them new life. Buying second hand doesn't just save money, it also helps the environment.

16. Green Franchises

Want to run a business with a solid brand and customer base already in place? Investing in a franchise might be the answer. While franchising might call to mind fast-food joints and hotel chains, there are many eco-friendly franchise businesses.

17. Secondhand Store

New things are typically expensive, and pretty soon, those costs add up. For example, a new book could cost $15 to $30, while a used book usually costs only a couple of dollars.

Opening a secondhand store not only saves your customers money, it's better for the environment. Instead of tossing a perfectly good item into the trash, encourage consumers to donate their used items to you so another person can get value out of that item. You can sell used clothes, coats, books, kitchen appliances, and furniture.

18. Green Consulting

Whether it's cutting energy costs or reducing their carbon footprint, the pressure for businesses to adopt green practices is high, and it's only going to grow.

Business sustainability consultant Barbara Englehart said there are numerous benefits for companies that go green, including reduced costs, risks and liabilities, and increased employee retention and productivity.

"This is all quite new in the business world, and companies need help," Englehart told Business News Daily. "They weren't teaching sustainability in business schools five or 10 years ago."

19. Solar Panel Installation

Many green-minded homeowners have installed solar panels on their homes, and many more would like. If you know how to do this, offer this service in your area.

20. Eco-friendly Cleaning

Common cleaning products contain chemicals that contribute to pollution and harm people and pets that come in contact with them. Starting an eco-friendly cleaning business counters this problem. Your eco-friendly cleaning business can exclusively use nontoxic products or use brands that minimize their use of single-use plastics. You can further decrease your company's environmental impact by reusing gray water whenever possible.

21. Reusable Plastic Bottles

Single-use plastics are indisputably a leading cause for concern among environmentalists. Offer people a way to drink water on the go without contributing to plastic pollution by launching a green industry business that designs, produces, and sells reusable plastic bottles. Explore using alternative materials such as metal or glass, bottles made from recycled plastic, or renewable plastics from materials like corn starch or sawdust.

22. Environmental Impact and Carbon Emissions Lessons

Many people aren't aware of just how much carbon emissions their daily activities produce and the impact those activities have on the environment. Offer classes to educate the public about how driving, using air conditioning in the summer, leaving lights on unnecessarily, flying, and other activities contribute to carbon emissions. You can also teach people how to reduce the environmental impact of these activities.

23. Local Eco-friendly Recycling Business

Chances are that your town's Department of Public Works oversees a public recycling program, but many experts say that what you put in your recycling bin doesn't always get recycled. Some municipalities don't accept all types of recyclable containers, while others may not thoroughly sort the collected recycling. Open

an eco-friendly local recycling business to guarantee
your community that their goods are recycled.

Whatever your business or organization, and whatever the size,
know that there is a place for sustainability in your operations.
Whether you have a green business, green products, or a "regular"
business that is simply run sustainably, you are making a difference.
You are reducing your environmental impact on the world, and that
matters. Give yourself (and your employees) a high-five. Well done
on the green choices you have made or will soon make. The world
thanks you.

Bibliography

Awair. 2019. 7 Real Estate Benefits of Green Building Certification. https://www.getawair.com/blog/7-real-estate-bene-fits-of-green-building-certification accessed 7/31/22

Babson College Green Purchasing Policy. https://www.babson.edu/business-and-financial-services/procurement/policies-and-pro-cedures/green-purchasing-policy/ accessed 7/23/22

Bell, Shelby. 2019. THE BENEFITS OF USING CENTRALIZED COLLECTION POINTS AT BUSINESSES. https://www.roadrun-nerwm.com/blog/centralized-collection-points accessed 4/6/22

Bhattacharya, CB, Sen, Sankar, and Korschun, Daniel. Leveraging Corporate Responsibility: The Stakeholder Route to Maximizing Business and Social Value, Cambridge, England: Cambridge University Press, 2011.

BHP (Broken Hill Proprietary Company Limited) Prospectus. 2018. https://www.bhp.com/-/media/documents/media/pros-pects/180824_prospects_understandingscope3footprintofour-valuechain.pdf?la=en#:~:text=Double%20counting%20in%20 scope%203,scope%203%20inventories%20they%20calculate. accessed 7/27/22

Business News Daily. 2022. Most Consumers Want Sustainable Products and Packaging. https://www.businessnewsdaily. com/15087-consumers-want-sustainable-products.html accessed 7/18/22

Carbonauts. https://www.thecarbonauts.com/

Clancy, Heather. 2012. Greenbiz. Verdantix offers a blueprint for green office buildings. accessed https://www.greenbiz.com/article/ver-dantix-offers-blueprint-green-office-buildings 7/31/22

Cone. 2016. https://conecomm.com/2016-employee-engage-ment-study/ accessed 5/22/22

Das, Prinona. 2021. What Is A Green Product? – Examples, Advantages, & Challenges. https://www.feedough.com/green-product/ accessed 7/31/22

Department of Environmental Protection (DEP), Commonwealth of Massachusetts. Health & Environmental Effects of Air Pollution. https://www.mass.gov/doc/health-environmental-ef-fects-of-air-pollution/download#:~:text=Air%20pollution%20can%20damage%20crops,(such%20as%20harsh%20weather) accessed 7/24/22

Endangered Species International. https://www.endangeredspe-ciesinternational.org/environcommit.html accessed 7/28/22

Environmental Protection Agency (EPA). Indoor Air Quality. https://www.epa.gov/indoor-air-quality-iaq/office-building-occupants-guide-indoor-air-quality accessed 5/29/22

Environmental Protection Agency (EPA). National Overview: Facts and Figures on Materials, Wastes and Recycling. https://www.epa.gov/facts-and-figures-about-materials-waste-and-recycling/

national-overview-facts-and-figures-materials#Landfilling accessed 7/24/22

Environmental Protection Agency (EPA). Offsets and RECs: What's the Difference? https://www.epa.gov/sites/default/files/2018-03/documents/gpp_guide_recs_offsets.pdf#view=fit accessed 7/21/22

Environmental Protection Agency (EPA). What is a Circular Economy? https://www.epa.gov/recyclingstrategy/what-circular-economy accessed 7/19/22

European Environment Agency. Ocean Acidification. https://www.eea.europa.eu/data-and-maps/indicators/ocean-acidification-2/assessment accessed 7/24/22

Freedman, Max. 2022. 23 Green Business Ideas for Eco-Minded Entrepreneurs. https://www.businessnewsdaily.com/5102-green-business-ideas.html accessed 7/31/22

Gangolells, Marta, Gaspar, Katia, Casals, Miquel, Ferré-Bigorra, Jaume, Forcada, Nuria, Macarulla, Marcel. 2020. Life-cycle environmental and cost-effective energy retrofitting solutions for office stock. Sustainable Cities and Society, Volume 61, https://doi.org/10.1016/j.scs.2020.102319. https://www.sciencedirect.com/science/article/pii/S2210670720305400 accessed 7/31/22

The Global Climate Pledge. https://www.globalclimatepledge.com/individual-pledge/ accessed 7/23/22

Green Business Bureau. 2021. Corporate Sustainability Training for Employees: An Executive Guide. https://greenbusinessbureau.com/business-function/executive/executive-guide/corporate-sustainability-training-an-executive-guide/#:~:text=Wherever%20your%20business%20lies%20in,well%20as%20cultivate%20behavior%20change. accessed 7/30/22

Green Business Bureau. The Sustainability Checklist: 25 Things To Do when Launching and Managing a Sustainability Program.

https://greenbusinessbureau.com/getting-started/the-sustainability-checklist-download/ accessed 3/15/22

Green Business Bureau. 2022. What Is Sustainable Marketing and Why Is It Important in 2022. https://greenbusinessbureau.com/business-function/marketing-sales/what-is-sustainable-marketing-and-why-is-it-important-in-2021/ accessed 5/22/22

Green Dot Bioplastics. 6 Tips to Make Your Products More Sustainable. https://www.greendotbioplastics.com/6-tips-to-make-your-products-more-sustainable/ accessed 7/18/22

Greenbiz. 2016. How sustainable cities can drive business growth. https://www.greenbiz.com/article/how-sustainable-cities-can-drive-business-growth accessed 7/15/22

Harris, Sam. 2019. Eco-Act. How to calculate a carbon footprint for your business. https://eco-act.com/carbon-reporting/how-to-calculate-a-carbon-footprint-for-your-business/ accessed 7/19/22

Heiskanen, Siru. 2016. https://www.naava.io/science/why-is-nature-beneficial-the-role-of-connectedness-to-nature?hsLang=en-us accessed 5/29/22

The Humane League. 2021. Effects of Deforestation on Humans and the Environment. https://thehumaneleague.org/article/effects-of-deforestation accessed 7/24/22

Inspire Clean Energy. 2021. Ways to Protect the Environment. https://www.inspirecleanenergy.com/blog/sustainable-living/ways-to-protect-the-environment accessed 7/14/22

International Energy Agency (IEA). 2019. Global Status Report for Buildings and Construction 2019. https://www.iea.org/reports/global-status-report-for-buildings-and-construction-2019 accessed 7/25/22

Interview with Ralf Pfitzner and Frank Klein. 2019. https://www.volk-swagenag.com/en/news/stories/2019/09/sustainability-is-becom-ing-increasingly-important-for-investors.html accessed 7/15/22

McCloy, John. 2019. Caring For The Environment: 8 Reasons to Protect & Sustain Earth. https://greencoast.org/caring-for-the-en-vironment/ accessed 7/31/22

Mission Blue. https://mission-blue.org/act-now/ accessed 7/24/22

Mylo. https://www.mylo-unleather.com/stories/what-is-my-celium/#:~:text=Most%20Common%20Uses%20of%20Mycelium&text=Mycelium%20can%20be%20used%20to,building%20materials%2C%20such%20as%20brick accessed 7/31/22

National Association of State Procurement Officials (NASPO). https://www.naspo.org/green-purchasing-guide/ accessed 3/25/22

National Environmental Education Foundation (NEEF). 2017. Winning in the Marketplace and the Workplace. https://www.neefusa.org/resource/winning-marketplace-and-workplace accessed 3/31/22

National Resources Defense Council (NRDC). What's at Stake. https://www.nrdc.org/food-waste accessed 7/24/22

Nicasio, Francesca. 2021. 9 Environmentally Friendly Packaging Materials to Help Your Business Go Green. https://noissue.co/blog/environmentally-friendly-packaging-materials/ accessed 7/22/22

NOAA Fisheries. 2022. Understanding Ocean Acidification. https://www.fisheries.noaa.gov/insight/understanding-ocean-acidifica-tion accessed 7/24/22

Pickup, Oliver. 2021. Worklife: How sustainability has become an advantage in the talent war, but candidates aren't fooled by 'greenwashing,' say experts. https://worklife.news/talent/

how-sustainability-has-become-an-advantage-in-the-talent-war-but-candidates-arent-fooled-by-greenwashing-say-experts/ accessed 3/14/22

Press8 Telecom. What is a Sustainability Policy and Why Your Company Needs One. https://www.press8.com/what-is-a-sustainability-policy-and-why-your-company-needs-one/ accessed 7/25/22

PWC. The future of work A journey to 2022: https://pwc.blogs.com/files/future-of-work-report-1.pdf accessed 3/14/22

Rachelson, David. 2018. In My Opinion: Circular economy metrics that matter most. Resource Recycling. https://resource-recycling.com/recycling/2018/09/05/in-my-opinion-circular-economy-metrics-that-matter-most/#:~:text=Diversion%2C%20a%20weight%2Dbased%20measurement,material%20diverted%20from%20the%20landfill accessed 3/30/22

Ritchie, Hannah and Roser, Max. 2021. Our World in Data. https://ourworldindata.org/air-pollution#air-pollution-is-one-of-the-world-s-leading-risk-factors-for-death accessed 7/24/22

Roop & Co. 2022. 3 Reasons To Include Sustainability In Your Marketing Strategy. https://roopco.com/marketing-sustainability/ accessed 5/22/22

S.1982 - Save Our Seas 2.0 Act. 2020. https://www.congress.gov/bill/116th-congress/senate-bill/1982/text accessed 7/18/22

SEC Proposes Rules to Enhance and Standardize Climate-Related Disclosures for Investors. 2022. https://www.sec.gov/news/press-release/2022-46 accessed 7/23/22

See Change Magazine. 2021. How Sustainability Measures Improve Employee Morale. https://www.seechangemagazine.com/how-sustainability-measures-improve-employee-morale/#:~:text=Employees'%20wellbeing%2C%20sense%20 of%20fulfillment,and%20happiness%20in%20the%20office accessed 5/22/22

Shad, Eric. 2020. 7 Positive Environmental Benefits of Remote Work https://www.virtualvocations.com/blog/telecommuting-survival/8-environmental-benefits-of-remote-work/ accessed 7/31/22

Stand for Trees. Death in the Forest: Deforestation Effects on Animals and What You Can Do. https://standfortrees.org/blog/deforestation-effects-on-animals/#:~:text=Deforestation%20affects%20animals%20in%20many,the%20main%20causes%20of%20extinction accessed 7/30/22

Tenney, Matt. How Important Sustainability Is To Employees. https://businessleadershiptoday.com/how-important-sustainability-is-to-employees/#:~:text=Sustainability%20is%20very%20important%20to,to%20the%20work%20they%20do accessed 5/22/22

Terrapass. 2020. Green Your Business: 10 Ways to Reduce Your Carbon Footprint. https://terrapass.com/blog/green-your-business-10-ways-to-reduce-your-carbon-footprint accessed 7/21/22

ThoughtCo. 2019. How Much Oxygen Does One Tree Produce? https://www.thoughtco.com/how-much-oxygen-does-one-tree-produce-606785#:~:text=%22A%20mature%20leafy%20tree%20produces,people%20inhale%20in%20a%20year.%22&text=%22A%20100%2Dfoot%20tree%2C,for%20a%20family%20of%20four.%22 accessed 7/24/22

UN Environment Programme. 2021. Methane emissions are driving climate change. https://www.unep.org/news-and-stories/story/methane-emissions-are-driving-climate-change-heres-how-reduce-them#:~:text=Methane%20is%20the%20primary%20contributor,at%20warming%20than%20carbon%20dioxide accessed 7/28/22

Unisan. 2022. What is a landfill? Why are landfills bad for the environment? https://www.unisanuk.com/what-is-a-landfill-why-are-landfills-bad-for-the-environment/#:~:text=The%20three%20main%20problems%20with,form%20leachate%20and%20landfill%20gas accessed 7/24/22

World Economic Forum. 2020. Circular economy examples - how IKEA, Burger King, Adidas and more are investing in a circular economy. https://www.weforum.org/agenda/2020/12/circular-economy-examples-ikea-burger-king-adidas/ accessed 7/22/22

World Wildlife Fund (WWF). The Effects of Deforestation. https://www.wwf.org.uk/learn/effects-of/deforestation accessed 7/24/22

Zujewski, Bill. 2022. Sustainability Statements: How To Write One That Resonates with Employees and Customers. https://greenbusinessbureau.com/business-function/executive/sustainability-statements/#:~:text=We%20are%20committed%20to%20a,the%20community%20we%20do%20business accessed 7/22/22

Book Club Questions:

1. What is the significance of the title? Did you find it meaningful? Why or why not? Did it convey the content well?

2. Would you have given the book a different title? If yes, what would your title be?

3. What were the most important takeaways from the book?

4. What did you think of the writing style and content structure of the book?

5. Were there any quotes (or passages) that stood out to you? Why?

6. What did you like most about the book? What did you like the least?

7. What do you think the author's goal was in writing this book? What ideas were they trying to illustrate? What message were they trying to send?

8. What did you learn from this book?

9. Would you recommend the book to a friend? How would you summarize the content if you were to recommend it?

10. If you could talk to the author, what burning question would you want to ask?

Author Bio:

Lael Giebel grew up in Berkeley, California, spent several years in Indonesia, and now lives in Central Florida with her husband and four sons. She is a sustainability professional, public speaker, and author. She has several industry certifications and an MBA in Sustainability. She writes straightforward, pragmatic works about the environment and how to integrate sustainability into your everyday life and business. When she's not reading (and any genre is fair game), she enjoys tending her chickens, ducks, and bees or taking nature walks with her family. You can find her on LinkedIn (https://www.linkedin.com/in/laelgiebel/).

More books from
Accomplishing Innovation Press

Workbooks

4HP Writer's Resources
The Author's Accountability Planner

The General Worldbuilding Guide
The Science Fiction Worldbuilding Guide
The Paranormal Worldbuilding Guide
The Romance Worldbuilding Guide
The Fantasy Worldbuilding Guide

Jörgen Jensen with Peter Lundgren
Mind Over Tennis: Mastering the Mental Game

Josh Stehle
I Am A Suphero Expert: Growing Up with my Autistic Brother

Kiyomi Holland
HeARTwork

Lael Giebel
Sustainability is for Everyone: Beginning Steps to Creating a Sustainability Program for Your Business

Letitia Washington
The Psychology of Character Building for Authors

Megan Mackie
Advanced Con Quest

N.B. Johnson
Wonders and Miracles

Valerie Willis
Writer's Bane: Research
Writer's Bane: Formatting 101
Writer's Bane: Plot & Foreshadowing
Writer's Bane: Revisions & Edition (w/ JM Paquette)
Writer's Bane: Character Development

Academia & Textbooks

Dr. Jenifer Paquette
Sentence Diagramming 101: Fun with Linguistics (and Movies)

Textbooks
Composition and Grammar: For HCC by HCC

Discover more at
ACCOMPLISHINGINNOVATIONPRESS.COM

CPSIA information can be obtained
at www.ICGtesting.com
Printed in the USA
LVHW101934230123
737762LV00021B/752/J